BOLD ITALIAN

Also by the author

New Italian Cooking

BROADWAY BOOKS NEW YORK

Fresh, new ways to coo

SCOTT CONANT

with JOANNE MCALLISTER SMART

Bold ITALIAN

inspired Italian dishes at home

PUBLISHED BY BROADWAY BOOKS

Copyright © 2007 by Scott Conant

All Rights Reserved

Published in the United States by Broadway Books,
an imprint of The Doubleday Broadway Publishing Group,
a division of Random House, Inc., New York.
www.broadwaybooks.com

BROADWAY BOOKS and its logo, a letter B bisected on the diagonal,
are trademarks of Random House, Inc.

Book design by Elizabeth Rendfleisch

Library of Congress Cataloging-in-Publication Data
Conant, Scott.
    Bold Italian : fresh, new ways to cook inspired Italian dishes at home /
by Scott Conant with Joanne Smart.
        p. cm.
    Includes index.
1. Cookery, Italian, I. Smart, Joanne McAllister. II. Title.

    TX723.C61725 2007
    641.5945—dc22

                                                                2007001758

ISBN 978-0-7679-1683-7

PRINTED IN CHINA

10 9 8 7 6 5 4 3 2 1

First Edition

For my beautiful, thoughtful, wonderful wife,

Meltem Bozkurt-Conant;

every day you make me feel like

the luckiest guy on earth. I love you!

CONTENTS

Acknowledgments

If I wrote every name of every person who has helped me get to the point of writing a second cookbook, there would be more names than recipes. If I have missed someone, know you are in my heart if not on paper.

I have had the fortune to have all the right people around me through all times in my life. I have to thank all of them for either the weeks or the years that they have aided in my growth, evolution, and well-being. In no particular order, they include John Nagler, Sergio Esposito, Jay Veduccio, Kevin Sippel, Atelio Ramos, Eduardo "Chepi" Cajamarca, Edwin Vega, Jorge Espinosa, Orlando Noralsco, Tim Butler, Gerry Minos, Prisca Nykolyszyn, Rachel Ossokow, Giovanni Gambrioni, Nadia Levin, Tom Black, Dr. and Mrs. Dattero, Mr. and Mrs. Vale, Djordje Stefanovic, Jory Wood, Andrew Essex, Craig Wallen, Syd Silverman, and Jonathan Schwartz.

To my lovely mother and father, who brought me into this world and allowed me to be my own person even when I wasn't ready for it—thank you for letting me leap.

My agent, Patricia Vanderleun, and my editor, Jennifer Josephy, who always seems to find a thread to make the ideas behind the book become more clear.

Thanks to Phillip Baltz and Sarah Abell.

My manager, lawyer, and good friend, Geoffrey Menin.

Tamar Davir Schulte

Scott Goldsmith

To my great friends, Shimon and Tammar, there is no space to describe the love and affection that I have for you both; thank you so much for the beautiful photographs in this book.

Thanks also to food stylist Jee Levine, who is just so good at what she does.

To Meg Suzuki for testing these recipes and never hesitating to be honest (sometimes brutally so) about the results.

Of course, thanks to writer Joanne Smart for getting my thoughts and recipes down on paper in a way that sounds remarkably like me. Thanks also to her family for letting me steal her away on many a Saturday—the only quiet day in my life—so we could cook and work together.

To all my customers: Thank you for your trust in me and my staff, for your feedback (both positive and negative), and for your caring about the state of the restaurants in general and my well-being in particular; it is all very touching.

And last but best, thanks to Steve Rubin; all I can say is that I love you and am so very fortunate to have you in my life. Thank you for being you.

Finally, to whoever is not on this list: please know that while my affection for you is limitless, the length of this page is not.

BOLD ITALIAN

Introduction

There is an urge you get when you're enjoying really good food. Whether it's a bowl of clams in a fragrant garlic broth, meltingly tender braised beef short ribs, or a perfectly roasted chicken surrounded by its own flavorful juices, you feel compelled to tear off a chunk of bread and mop up any remaining sauce. The Italians, God bless them, actually have a word for this: *scarpetta.* It literally means "little shoe," and it refers to the shape the bread takes on when it's poised for action between your fingers. *Scarpetta* is something I keep in mind whenever I am creating a new dish for one of my restaurants. While I want my food to be bold and exciting—what chef doesn't?—it's just as important that my cooking satisfies on that instinctual, primal level. It has to feed the hunger in your belly as well as the hunger in your soul. While such words as *innovative* and *intellectual* have been used to describe my cooking, it pleases me more when I hear my food called simple and honest.

What do I mean by those words? By *simple,* I don't mean that all of my recipes are easy to make, although you'll see as you peruse this collection that many of them are. *Simple* refers less to the process than to the final result. No matter what the recipe entails, no matter how many ingredients it requires, what winds up on the plate, while exciting and flavorful, is also easy to "get." There's no taking a bite and wondering: "Do I like this?" With each bite, the dish becomes more exciting as different layers of flavors are uncovered and revealed, but it always maintains that inherent simplicity.

As for the word *honest,* I use it a lot when I talk about my cooking, and honesty has a hand in keeping my recipes simple. As a chef trying to make a name for yourself, it can be easy to get caught up in creating dishes that are meant to show off your flair, your creativity, even your bravery. I try to get out a lot to sample what my colleagues are cooking, and much of the time their offerings leave me wanting. The dishes feel more contrived than comforting; they may please on an academic level, but they don't gratify emotionally. While it's important that we chefs introduce people to new flavor concepts, new ingredients, and new ways of presentation, the recipes themselves have to stand on their own as something people really *want* to eat. The way some chefs push the envelope, contorting ingredients unrecognizably, often feels more forced than fulfilling. When I eat this kind of food, I feel like I'm being dared, not fed; often I wonder if the chef himself really enjoys it.

As I begin working on a new menu, I think about the season, and I think about a particular ingredient and what would naturally pair well with it. I make a list of main ingredients on one side of a piece of paper—lamb shanks, veal chops, peas, asparagus, razor clams—and a long list of flavorings and accompaniments on the other—chickpeas, crispy shallots, fennel, truffle—you get the idea. I then draw lines from the items on the left side to those on the right until I end up with what looks like a hyperactive first grader's matching worksheet. While I strive for inspired combinations, what matters most during this brainstorming is letting the natural expression of the ingredients be my guide. In this way, I know that I am keeping my cooking honest.

By now you may be wondering what is so bold about my cooking. I believe it's the fact that I, along with a handful of other chefs around the country, am changing people's perceptions about what Italian food—and specifically, Italian-*American* food—can be. I take Italy as a starting point, absolutely, but I also never forget that I am cooking in America; and more specifically, that I am cooking in New York City. The resulting recipes are neither the homey, Italian-American fare we all grew up with, nor are they the precious, region-specific cuisine to which some Italian restaurants (safely) hold fast. Instead, my food celebrates, translates, and updates dishes from the various regions of Italy, all the while being filtered through my own personal experience.

To step outside of convention, you not only have to be bold, but you also have to really believe in what you're doing (or cooking, in this case). And at times, my style of cooking has confused both diners and critics. Although they liked it, they didn't agree on exactly what it was. It helps that magazines like *Wine Spectator* have since been educating people on this new wave of Italian cooking in America. But ultimately, what puts people most at ease is the food itself.

As for the food, much of it will, in fact, feel familiar. Recipes for pasta, polenta, and risotto are all featured at my restaurants as well as in this book. So, too, are many classic Italian ingredients: olive oil, garlic, rosemary, tomatoes, Parmigiano-Reggiano. If some dishes seem a little less familiar, such as the stuffed pasta called *plin* (page 100), it may be because these dishes hail from the very north of Italy, which in the past has gotten less attention than the south in the restaurant world. I draw a lot of inspiration from this northern region—specifically Alto Adige, which abuts Austria—and indeed spent a lot of time there while on a cooking internship in nearby Germany. You'll spot this northern influence in recipes that feature plenty of cold-resistant vegetables like cabbage, carrots, onions, and beets. Plus potatoes, lots of them. And dumplings and spaetzle, too.

But whether I'm cooking with a northern Italian accent or a more southern Italian style, for me the phrase *Italian cooking* signifies a purity of flavor, a respect for natural ingredients, and perhaps most of all, an innate understanding of how to create a dish that makes people want to reach for a hunk of bread to wipe up the last bits on the plate. I begin with a deep understanding of and passion for the ingredients and notions behind the best of true Italian cooking. The understanding comes from watching and helping my Neapolitan grandmother in the kitchen; the passion comes from extended travel and study throughout Italy. Every year, I spend at least a month there, not only experiencing the classic traditional dishes of the various regions, but also visiting innovative, forward-thinking chefs to see how they create a balance between the known and beloved and the new and exciting.

When I get back to New York, always a few pounds heavier than I'd like, I go into the kitchen and let inspiration take over. I tweak and change the cuisine I just experienced there in a way that I know will stimulate and satisfy my customers here. None of my recipes may be exactly and traditionally Italian, and indeed they may seem completely novel, but they all have an Italian soul. That sounds a little kooky, I know, but once you start enjoying these recipes, I think you will understand.

FAVORITE INGREDIENTS, METHODS, AND TOOLS

When assembling a collection of recipes, certain patterns and themes become evident as they repeat themselves in various ways in different recipes. Every chef has favorite ingredients that get used over and over again. Rosemary, thyme, and garlic, not surprisingly, are my aromatic favorites. I often use whole sprigs of the herbs (and by "whole sprig" I mean a piece about four inches long), to infuse flavor. Shallot and crushed red pepper—I call it by its Italian name, *peperoncino,* in my kitchen—wind up in many dishes, too. I love the subtle sweetness the shallot imparts and the hint of heat from the pepper. Because red pepper's intensity can vary widely and is affected by age—how long it's been sitting in your spice rack—and because people have differing tolerances for heat (I tend toward spicy myself), I usually give a range for how much to use. Start with the lesser amount and add more "to taste."

I'm also on a truffle kick these days. I don't necessarily want the flavor in the foreground, but I often finish a dish with a little preserved truffle or good-quality truffle oil for the added depth it offers. You don't immediately think truffle, you only think yum. I know good-quality preserved truffles can be a bit of a splurge, but they're a bargain compared to fresh. (Though if you do get your hands on a fresh truffle, shave a little over grilled bread brushed with olive oil and a smidge of sea salt—heaven.) To make preserved truffles taste even better, remove them from the oil they came in and pour some good-quality olive oil over them. (Use that oil, too.)

When cooking with truffle oil, you really need only a few *drops* per dish, which means you can purchase a teeny, tiny bottle of really good stuff. (Poor-quality truffle oils taste synthetic.) In fact, you should buy only a very small bottle because exposure to light, heat, and air affects the flavor of truffle oil (as it does all oils), which means a larger bottle may decline in quality before you are through using it. Another option is to use the truffle oil that the preserved truffles are packed in.

As for olive oil, I use extra virgin olive oil exclusively because I find it easier for my line cooks to reach for a single style of oil as they cook. For sautéing and searing, however, you don't have to use extra virgin; the flavor of the olive oil when it's cooked gets dissipated, so a regular olive oil will work fine. However, when you are adding olive oil to something uncooked, such as a vinaigrette, or to something warm, as in the olive oil I add to my pureed soups, use extra virgin. Olive oils can vary greatly in flavor from hot and peppery to florally herbaceous to green and grassy. Buy a few different kinds to see which you like best. You may even find that you like different olive oils for different uses, such as a mild one to accent pea soup and a more pungent one to slather on grilled bread.

Salt is another ingredient that is fun to sample and experiment with. For all of my cooking, I use kosher salt. In pasta cooking water, it dissolves more quickly, leaving no chemical aftertaste. When seasoning meat, you can actually see the larger grains, which helps you season properly. Kosher salt also does not taste overtly salty. For finishing dishes, I reach for sea salt. I'll play around with various kinds, from a gray *sel de mer* to a smoked salt on raw oysters, but my favorite for finishing just about every dish is the widely available Maldon sea salt. The crystals in this additive-free salt are flaked. Though they provide a distinctive texture, they're actually quite soft—when you bite down on the crystals, they immediately give in. (Some sea salts can be quite hard on the teeth.) And instead of obscuring the flavor of the steak, salad, or fish, the salt works to bring out the flavor of the food. As with truffle oil, a little goes a long way.

When finishing a dish, add just the tiniest of pinches. My advice is to keep a salt cellar filled with this sea salt near the stove or on the table. Once you start using it (if you don't already), you will understand how this easiest of culinary "tricks" is often what takes a dish from good to great.

Cheese is one of my favorite foods, and something I don't like to skimp on. Seek out a good cheese shop; it's worth your time and the extra gas money to patronize a shop that handles cheese properly—no plastic-wrapped blue cheeses, please—and hires knowledgeable staff. For the king of Italian cheese, Parmigiano-Reggiano, be sure you are buying the real thing; its name will be stenciled in large letters on the rind if it's the real deal, properly aged and produced in the designated region. Domestic "Parmesan" won't cut it; better to go with imported, good-quality grana Padano if you're looking to save a few bucks.

A cheese I discovered a few years back, and which has recently become the cheese darling of many chefs, is burrata, a specialty cheese from Puglia. Made by combining fresh cream with mozzarella curds that have not been spun, these decadent balls ooze with a creamy richness once they meet a knife. I feature burrata as part of my cheese course, and also use it to great success in my cannelloni (page 94). The good news about its popularity is that it's becoming easier to get your hands on. (The bad news is that what was once special at my restaurant is being widely duplicated at other restaurants; so it goes . . .) Nothing can compare to burrata when eaten out of hand, but you could replace it in, say, the cannelloni with a good-quality fresh ricotta, preferably one made with buffalo milk.

Certain techniques and processes also recur regularly in my cooking. As I worked with my recipe tester, I found myself describing how to cook everything from a rib eye to a large piece of fish to a veal chop in the same way, "You know the routine—sear on the stove, finish in the oven." This sear-roasting is a time-honored process used by many professional chefs, mainly because stove space is at such a premium. However, my method differs in that instead of finishing, say, lamb chops quickly in a very hot oven, I finish them more slowly in a very, very low oven. The main reason for using this technique is that the slow cooking relaxes the muscle of the protein so that it becomes tender and cooks evenly. Another benefit—this method is practically foolproof as it's almost impossible to overcook anything this way. Plus, in the 15 to 20 minutes the steak takes to finish, you can get the rest of the meal together. One potential drawback, however, is that the food comes out less than piping hot, so it's crucial to have the dinner plates very warm, almost hot.

Smaller fish fillets get sautéed in minutes on the stove. To keep the fish from sticking and the delicate flakes from breaking, I use quite a lot of oil and get the pan very hot. Instead of lifting the fish out of the pan to turn it over, I use a spoon to turn it onto one edge, then let it fall back into the hot oil.

I think one of the biggest mistakes made in home cooking is underseasoning. Salt has gotten a bad rap, so people tend to avoid it. But if you don't add salt as you cook, what you make will ultimately lack flavor. Also, it's important to season as you go, adding a little salt to the aromatics you're combining before other ingredients are added. Begin with a little bit of salt and pepper, especially for long-cooking foods, as the flavor of all of the ingredients will intensify during the course of cooking. You can always add more salt, but it's impossible to remove it.

Two other processes I use often are blanching and pureeing. Blanching vegetables—boiling them briefly until just barely tender and cooling them quickly—before adding them to a dish allows for more control. Blanching lets you brown vegetables easily; they're done as soon as their exterior is browned. Blanched vegetables can also be added at the last minute to a braise or soup; this way they keep their shape and don't become overcooked. In pasta dishes, I love the accent of tiny diced vegetables, all of which retain their unique flavor if they are blanched separately. Though the blanching step can make a recipe look tedious, especially with multiple vegetables, the process is so quick and clean—there's just a pot of water to rinse—that once you're in the habit of blanching, you won't mind it at all.

My love of pureeing began with soup. You cook up a pot of vegetables and broth, throw them in a blender, and, presto, you have a full-flavored soup. I usually add ample olive oil to my purees to emulsify them and give them a wonderful creamy consistency without the cream. My soups inspired the use of purees to create intensely flavorful, healthful sauces for pasta, fish, and meat. Almost all purees can be made ahead, so all you need to add a dramatic touch to a plate is to gently reheat the puree and spoon it on.

A good blender can make all the difference in how much you enjoy pureeing. I can't imagine cooking without my Vita-Mix blender. Though more expensive than most brands, it's a good investment and something to consider if you make a lot of pureed soups and smoothies. The blade will get through just about anything and its square bottom means there's no clogging of ingredients. Its powerful motor will last a home cook forever, and its large capacity eliminates the annoying "puree in batches" business that most blenders and food processors require. If you don't go with a Vita-Mix, you may as well consider a handheld blender. It doesn't puree as well as the Vita-Mix, but with the handheld model you get decent results combined with the ability to puree the soup or sauce right in the pot.

Other tools I can't live without include my tongs, sharp knives, and heavy-based pans, such as stainless steel and cast iron, that can go from stove to oven. A squared-off wooden spoon is my favorite for stirring risotto. A spider or Chinese skimmer works better than a slotted spoon for retrieving foods from hot oil or water because the larger holes drain more of the liquid.

In the pastry kitchen, we often use round, bottomless molds for creating individual desserts. (Cleaned tuna fish cans with their bottoms and tops removed are a good substitute.) A Silpat, a reusable silicone baking sheet liner, is another handy item, though you can also use parchment paper to keep foods from sticking. If you really enjoy making ice cream—and you will once you try the gelato on page 218—consider a countertop version of an ice cream maker, which means you don't have to plan ahead and freeze the ice cream bucket, as most models require.

Finally, thoughtfully consider your serving plates. Explore different plate shapes, something I do at my restaurant. When you're taking something familiar (in this case, Italian food) and expanding on that familiarity, the presentation is very important. Italian food has often been known as a certain thing, and my goal, as I hope you understand if you have read this far, is to push that perception a little bit. Some of the dish is familiar, but the presentation tells you that the food has moved far beyond what you'd assume is Italian. If you serve your risotto on a square plate, for example, you are hinting at a new culinary experience before the food is even tasted. Regardless of which shape plate you use, however, always choose white. After all, it's the color of the food, and not the plate, that should be noticed.

A few basic cooking terms are used over and over. Instead of defining them for each recipe, I have made the following list, not only for easy reference, but also to let you know exactly what I mean when I employ these words and phrases. Unless otherwise stated in the recipe, these definitions and techniques apply.

BLANCH: *Blanch* means to cook a food (usually vegetables) in boiling water until just barely tender, and then halt the cooking by plunging it into an ice bath. This step can be done well in advance of using the ingredient in the final preparation.

BUNCH: I mainly use this word in reference to herbs, such as parsley or basil, and only when an exact amount won't matter much. The bunch I picture is a bouquet no bigger than my outstretched hand.

CARAMELIZE: This term technically refers to the browning of foods that contain sugars. However, it's often used when discussing meats. Basically, it means bringing a food to a rich, toasty, darkened state.

CHIFFONADE: This is a pretty and easy way to thinly slice basil and a few other large-leafed herbs. To make a chiffonade, stack a few leaves, roll them into a tight cylinder, and slice thinly crosswise with a very sharp knife.

CHOPPED, FINELY CHOPPED: This describes how to cut something when looks don't matter, such as when vegetables will be pureed. Plain old chopped usually means ¼- to ⅓-inch pieces; finely chopped, less than ¼-inch.

COARSELY CHOPPED: In general this means chopping an ingredient into 1- to 1 ½-inch pieces. For smaller ingredients, such as garlic cloves, it means cutting into fourths or sixths.

DICED, FINELY DICED: *Dice* means to carefully cut into cubes, about ¼ inch square for diced and ⅛ inch for finely diced.

EMULSIFY: Technically, this means getting two ingredients that don't normally mix, such as oil and vinegar, to bind. The connotation is that the overall texture will become a little thicker and satiny, which is why I like to create emulsions in my risotto and my pureed soups by adding olive oil to them.

GRATED, FINELY GRATED: When something is to be grated, use the larger holes of your grater. For finely grated, use the smaller holes or a Microplane, which will yield very light and fluffy results.

JULIENNE: Cut into matchstick-size pieces.

NUTS, TOASTED: To get nuts nicely golden brown, either heat them on a baking sheet in a 400°F oven for up to 10 minutes, depending on size, or toss over medium- to medium-high heat in a dry skillet (especially convenient for tiny pine nuts). Watch carefully and check often to prevent burning. This step can be done well in advance of the final preparation.

PINCH: A pinch is somewhere between ⅛ and ¼ teaspoon.

SEASON WELL: When I use this phrase, it's usually in conjunction with a piece of meat or fish. I am most often referring to salt (kosher, not table) and, less often, pepper. For that initial seasoning, I use about ¼ teaspoon of salt per serving and about half that amount of pepper.

SHAVINGS: Shavings refer to longish paper-thin shards of cheese (and sometimes chocolate) made with a vegetable peeler, grater, or truffle slicer. Usually used as a garnish and done right over the serving plate.

SIMMER: This term can be confusing because on many stoves, the simmer setting is the lowest heat level (more like a "keep warm" setting). When I mean simmer, I mean that the food is still cooking but more gently. For liquids, it means just under a boil, with tiny bubbles gently coming to the surface.

SPRIG: In my recipes, a sprig is a branch from an herb measuring between 3 and 4 inches long. Some herbs, such as thyme, may include a few thin branches within one sprig.

TEMPER: This is the process of adding a hot ingredient to a cool ingredient a little at a time so as not to cook the cool one. The word is more often used by my pastry chef when he's making gelato or a custard.

THINLY SLICED, VERY THINLY SLICED: Thinly sliced in my mind falls between ⅛ inch and ³⁄₁₆ inch thick. Very thinly sliced means as thin as you can slice something while still keeping it in one piece, which requires a very sharp knife, mandoline, vegetable peeler, or truffle slicer.

TO TASTE: Seasonings, most often salt and pepper, are added until the flavor suits your palate. I suggest adding crushed red pepper flakes, lemon, and vinegar to taste as well.

WELL BROWNED: Well-browned food is cooked until uniformly darkened. People tend to err by underbrowning, which does not impart as much flavor. The best browning comes when you leave the food undisturbed in the hot pan for the time it takes to brown.

Piattini

Exhilaration. Invigoration. Anticipation. These big words describe what I'm after when I create my little plates—*piattini*—or appetizers. My goal: to wake up the palate, excite the senses (all of them), and create anticipation for the meal to come. For these reasons I often turn to seafood to create a dish that will launch a meal on the right note. With their inherent saltiness and some sweetness, you almost can't go wrong with dishes inspired by the sea. Because seafood tends to be lighter, you can have a few oysters, a bowlful of clams, a softshell crab, or some shrimp and not feel full.

Other tricks that we chefs use to tease appetites include featuring acidic flavors, like lemon and tomato; briny elements, like olives and capers; and in some cases, a little heat. In the right hands, even fried foods can feel light enough to enjoy as a starter. *Fritto misto*, for example, is a "mixed fry" that can be very heavy. In creating a version to serve as an appetizer, however (page 23), I add lemon slices and whole herb leaves, which make the dish taste bright and light. Similarly, my pan-fried, breaded mozzarella (Mozzarella in Carrozza, page 18) has a delicate coating and gets paired with a fresh, chunky tomato sauce. Sweet scallops get a peppery kick from well-cooked leeks (page 34), and the best-quality beef is served raw as a tartare topped with quickly pickled mushrooms (page 20).

Put these out for a party along with some cheese and cured meats and you're good to go.

ROSEMARY-SCENTED OLIVES MAKES ABOUT 2 CUPS

I am a big fan of these olives. Heating them with the rosemary and garlic expands their flavor while muting the somewhat harsh flavors some olives have.

2 cups mixed olives, rinsed and drained

2 tablespoons extra virgin olive oil

2 small fresh rosemary sprigs

2 garlic cloves, crushed

Pinch of crushed red pepper flakes
  (more if you're feeling sassy)

In a small saucepan, combine the olives, olive oil, rosemary, garlic, and red pepper flakes. Heat over medium-low heat, tossing occasionally, for 10 minutes. Let cool to room temperature and serve, or refrigerate for up to a week.

EGGPLANT CAPONATA MAKES ABOUT 2^1/2 CUPS

I make my caponata by frying the eggplant separately and then adding the sauce to it. Made like this, the eggplant keeps its distinct flavor, and how "stewy" the caponata turns out is easier to control. Serve at room temperature as a dip with grilled bread or toasted pita. Caponata will keep for a few days refrigerated and tastes even better a day or two after being made.

SALT THE EGGPLANT   Put the eggplant in a colander and toss with the teaspoon of salt. Put the colander in a clean sink, weight the eggplant, and allow the salt to draw out the excess moisture for 30 to 40 minutes.

MAKE THE SAUCE   Meanwhile, heat the 2 tablespoons of olive oil in a medium saucepan over medium heat. Add the onion, garlic, capers, red pepper flakes, and a pinch of salt. Sauté until the onion is tender and light brown, about 7 minutes. Add the tomato sauce and oregano and stir to combine well. Reduce the heat to low, cover the pan, and cook until the sauce reduces somewhat and the flavors have melded, about 20 minutes.

FRY THE EGGPLANT   Pat the salted eggplant dry. In a large, high-sided sauté pan, heat about ¼ inch of olive oil over medium-high heat. Fry the eggplant in batches, adding just enough to form one layer with room between the cubes, and stirring occasionally, until well browned and tender, 7 to 10 minutes per batch. Add more oil as needed between batches; eggplant soaks up olive oil like a sponge.

TO FINISH   Add the basil to the tomato sauce and stir. Return all of the eggplant to the sauté pan over low heat. Add just enough of the tomato sauce to the eggplant to create a stewy mixture. (Any leftover tomato sauce can be saved and served over pasta.) Taste and season with additional salt if needed. Toss in the pine nuts just before serving.

1 eggplant (about 1 pound), cut into 1-inch cubes to yield about 2^1/2 cups

1 teaspoon kosher salt, plus more for seasoning

2 tablespoons extra virgin olive oil, plus more for frying

1 small onion, diced

2 garlic cloves, thinly sliced

1 tablespoon capers, preferably salt-packed, well rinsed

Pinch of crushed red pepper flakes

1^1/2 cups good-quality tomato sauce (or use my Fresh Tomato Sauce, page 122)

1 teaspoon chopped fresh oregano

10 fresh basil leaves, cut into a chiffonade

^{1}/4 cup toasted pine nuts

MOZZARELLA IN CARROZZA WITH CHERRY TOMATO SAUCE SERVES 4

This crispy, fried mozzarella dish brings me back to Naples, where you buy mozzarella in carrozza on the street and eat it from a cone made of rolled paper. If I'm making these with panko, the Japanese-style bread crumbs that I often use, I give the panko a whirl in the food processor to grind it more finely. Serve these with the chunky Cherry Tomato Sauce that follows or with your favorite marinara. Lightly dressed baby greens would make a nice addition to the plate, too.

12 bocconcini or 2 regular-size balls fresh mozzarella (about 1 pound), drained

1 cup very fine dry bread crumbs

$1/4$ cup flour, more if needed

1 large egg

$1/2$ cup extra virgin olive oil, plus more if needed

Kosher salt

Cherry Tomato Sauce (recipe follows)

COAT THE MOZZARELLA   Cut the bocconcini in half or slice the larger balls ½ inch thick. Put the bread crumbs and flour on two separate plates. Crack the egg into a bowl and lightly beat it. Dip the mozzarella slices first in the flour, then the egg, and finally in the bread crumbs, making sure they are evenly coated. Place each coated piece on a baking sheet. Fry right away or chill for up to 24 hours.

FRY THE CHEESE   In a large sauté pan over medium-high heat, heat enough olive oil to come almost halfway up the sides of the mozzarella. When the oil is hot enough to make a few bread crumbs dropped into the pan sizzle, fry the mozzarella on one side until golden, about 2 minutes. (You'll likely need to do this in two batches.) Turn the mozzarella over and cook until golden on the other side, another 2 minutes. Season with salt to taste.

TO SERVE   Top with warm Cherry Tomato Sauce and some lightly dressed greens on the side, if you like.

CHERRY TOMATO SAUCE

MAKES ABOUT 1^1/$_2$ CUPS

When I want a chunky tomato sauce, I reach for sweet yet meaty cherry tomatoes.

2 tablespoons extra virgin olive oil

1 shallot, thinly sliced

1 pint cherry tomatoes, cut in half

^{1}/$_4$ to ^{1}/$_2$ cup chicken broth

6 fresh basil leaves, cut into a chiffonade

^{1}/$_2$ teaspoon fresh oregano leaves

Pinch of crushed red pepper flakes

Kosher salt

Heat the olive oil in a medium sauté pan over medium heat. Add the shallot and cook until tender, about 5 minutes. Add the tomatoes and cook, stirring occasionally, until they are just soft, 5 to 10 minutes. Add a little chicken broth to help create a more saucelike texture. Add the basil, oregano, and red pepper flakes and season with a little salt. If using right away, reduce to a simmer and keep warm. Otherwise, you can refrigerate the tomatoes and reheat them when you're ready to serve them.

BEEF TARTARE SERVES 4 TO 6

I usually make this with Wagyu beef, which is predisposed to marbling and so is rich and tender like Kobe beef, which comes from the same breed of cattle. Prime would work well, too. The shimeji mushrooms that garnish the tartare are becoming much more widely available; you'll likely see them packaged as they grow, with many tiny capped mushrooms emerging from a single stump.

1/4 cup extra virgin olive oil

16 to 20 shimeji mushroom caps plus a little stem (or other Japanese mushrooms, such as matsutake or shiitake), trimmed and sliced

1 teaspoon red wine vinegar

1 pound prime-grade beef tenderloin

1 tablespoon finely chopped preserved black truffles or 2 teaspoons good-quality truffle oil

1 tablespoon finely chopped fresh chives

Sea salt

1 ounce Parmigiano-Reggiano

SAUTÉ THE MUSHROOMS   Heat a teaspoon of the olive oil in a small sauté pan and sauté the mushrooms for just a few minutes over medium-high heat. Reduce the heat and sprinkle the vinegar over the mushrooms. Continue to cook another couple of minutes. Transfer to a small bowl or plate to cool.

MAKE THE TARTARE   Slice the beef thinly and then chop the slices into as fine a dice as you can. (For easier slicing, partially freeze the beef and use a very sharp knife.) Combine the meat with the remaining olive oil, the preserved truffles, and the chives. Season to taste with sea salt.

TO SERVE   Divide the tartare among serving plates. Top each serving with some pickled mushrooms and a few shavings of Parmigiano; serve immediately.

HERB- AND GARLIC-INFUSED TOMATOES

SERVES 6 AS AN APPETIZER OR A SIDE DISH

These tomatoes serve many purposes. Presented on some grilled or toasted bread, they make a tasty bruschetta. They are also a perfect side dish for lamb; their upfront herb and garlic flavors combined with the tomatoes' acidity counter that meat's gaminess nicely. I can also see them over a bowl of Creamy Polenta (page 173) or simply tossed with pasta. Save the oil the tomatoes cook in—it's delicious brushed on steak—but be sure to refrigerate it and use it within a week.

GENTLY COOK THE TOMATOES   Combine the tomatoes, thyme, rosemary, garlic, and red pepper flakes in a medium sauté pan. Add enough oil to submerge the tomatoes about halfway. Season with a few pinches of kosher salt. Heat over low heat until the tomatoes expand as much as possible without splitting (it's okay if a couple of them do), about 30 minutes. Take them off the heat. The tomatoes are delicious when served warm but will keep, refrigerated, for up to a week.

TO SERVE   Brush the bread with some of the flavored oil from the tomatoes and toast under the broiler or on a grill. Top with the tomatoes and serve.

3 cups cherry tomatoes

8 small fresh thyme sprigs

5 small fresh rosemary sprigs

5 garlic cloves, thinly sliced

Large pinch of crushed red pepper flakes

1 cup extra virgin olive oil, plus more if needed

Kosher salt

Slices of Italian bread, ciabatta, or baguette

LIGHT AND CRISPY FRITTO MISTO WITH FRIED LEMONS AND HERBS SERVES 4

With *fritto misto,* which means "mixed fry," Italians embrace a well-known cooking truism: Everything tastes good fried. My version features calamari, baby artichokes, and zucchini, which get fried after a quick dip in well-seasoned flour. What makes this dish outstanding are the thin slices of lemon and garlic and the whole leaves of rosemary and parsley that also get tossed into the roiling pot. When you bite into the lemon, it immediately banishes the notion that fried fare is heavy. The herbs, meanwhile, offer crunchy texture as well as bright flavor. (The parsley, which looks relatively unchanged after frying, nonetheless delicately crumbles as you bite it, making it addictively fun to eat.)

Just so you know: I never cut my squid into rings because I want to dispel immediately any recollections of greasy, heavy-handed calamari. Cut into thin little strips, the squid feels familiar but also more refined, frying up very delicately. When serving this, skip the plates and present the *fritto misto* right on a clean linen or kitchen towel; not only does this look sexy, but the towel will blot up the scant excess oil. This is a dish to serve to guests right in the kitchen with a glass of chilled Prosecco.

HEAT THE OIL   Fill a large, heavy-based saucepan about halfway with oil. Begin to heat the oil over medium heat, but don't let it get ripping until you have everything else ready to go.

PREPARE THE SQUID AND VEGETABLES   Separate the bodies and tentacles of the squid. If the squid are big, cut the tentacles in half; otherwise leave them whole. Cut the squid bodies open so they lie flat. With a sharp knife, cut them into strips about ¼ inch wide and 1½ inches long. Soak the strips in the milk while you prepare the vegetables.

Trim the stems and remove the outer leaves from the artichokes. Slice them very thinly through the stem end. (If you have true baby artichokes, you don't have to worry about the choke; if you can only find older artichokes, remove the spiny choke before slicing.)

(continued)

2 to 3 quarts peanut, grapeseed, or other vegetable oil

4 cleaned whole squid, about 1 pound

1 cup whole milk

6 baby artichokes

1 medium zucchini

1½ cups all-purpose flour

2 teaspoons kosher salt, plus more for seasoning

1 teaspoon freshly ground black pepper

2 lemons, 1 sliced very thin, the other cut into wedges

3 garlic cloves, sliced very thin

1 large handful fresh parsley leaves, washed and dried well, plus chopped parsley

1 small handful fresh rosemary leaves

Trim the ends off the zucchini and cut lengthwise into ¼-inch slices. From those slices, cut sticks about 1½ inches long.

SET UP YOUR FRY STATION   On a sheet pan or large platter, combine the flour, salt, and pepper. Have the sliced lemon, garlic, parsley, and rosemary prepared and nearby. Line plates or a platter with paper towels or parchment paper.

Increase the heat of the oil until it reaches 375°F on a candy/frying thermometer. Meanwhile, drain the squid and toss it, the artichokes, and the zucchini in the flour. Shake the flour pan back and forth quickly to help coat everything evenly.

FRY THE SQUID AND VEGETABLES   Once the oil is hot, fry the vegetables and squid, working in batches to keep the oil's temperature constant and prevent the oil from overflowing. Add about one-third of the vegetables and squid, plus a few of the lemon and garlic slices, and let cook for about 1 minute. Add about a third of the rosemary and the parsley and continue to cook until the vegetables and squid are a light golden brown, another 1 to 2 minutes. Using a spider or a Chinese strainer (or as a last resort, a traditional slotted spoon), transfer the fried foods to the lined plate.

TO SERVE   Season with more salt and chopped parsley and have the lemon wedges nearby for those who want to squeeze a little juice over the squid. This is best served hot, so let your guests dig in while you immediately begin cooking the next batch.

NOTE   While this is a great combination of flavors, don't hesitate to try (or should I say fry?) your own favorites. Just be sure to cut the food into similar-size pieces so they cook at the same rate.

CLAMS GUAZZETTO SERVES 2

Guazzetto means to slow-cook or simmer, usually with tomatoes and broth, in order to concentrate flavors—and that's exactly what goes on in this quick and easy dish. Best of all, as you finish up a good *guazzetto,* a flavorful, light broth should still cover the bottom of the bowl. Have some good crusty bread handy to sop it up. Manila clams look sexy (and taste sweet, too), but you can use any small hard-shell clam.

In a large saucepan or sauté pan with a lid, heat the olive oil over medium-high heat. Add the garlic, remove from heat, and let it sizzle off the heat for a minute. Add the tomatoes, return the pan to the heat, and cook, stirring occasionally, until the tomatoes release some of their juices. Add the broth and the clams. Cover the pan and cook, tossing once or twice, until the clams open, 5 to 7 minutes. Sprinkle the parsley over the clams, toss, and serve.

2 tablespoons extra virgin olive oil

2 or 3 garlic cloves, very thinly sliced

$^1/_2$ cup cherry tomatoes, cut in half

$^1/_2$ cup Chicken Broth (page 241)

36 Manila or other small hard-shell clams

1 tablespoon chopped fresh parsley

OYSTERS WITH BLOOD ORANGE, CHILE OIL, AND SMOKED SEA SALT SERVES 4

Some people find the idea of adding even a squeeze of lemon juice to an oyster sacrilege. I can understand that; a crisp raw oyster is a beautiful thing. But here the tiniest bit of sweetly acidic blood orange plus a hint of smoke and heat from the salt and red pepper oil work together to make the oyster's refreshing flavor even more vibrant. The trick is to be super stingy with the accompaniment—a little goes along way.

1 blood orange or other sweet orange, such as Mandarin

24 raw oysters, shucked

Smoked sea salt

Chile Oil (recipe follows) or good-quality purchased chile oil

SEGMENT THE ORANGE   Cut both ends off the orange. Using a sharp, flexible knife and a sawing motion, cut away the skin and membrane from top to bottom, following the contours. Free the segments from the fruit by cutting along the seams that separate one segment from the other. Cut the segments into ¼-inch pieces.

TO SERVE   Arrange 6 oysters per person on each serving plate. Top each with a few orange pieces, a tiny pinch of sea salt, and 2 drops of the hot oil. Serve immediately.

If you don't feel up to shucking oysters, have your fishmonger do it for you; just be careful to transport them home without spilling that beautiful oyster liquor and use them that same day.

CHILE OIL

MAKES 1 CUP

You will get much more flavor in this oil if you don't use an ancient jar of crushed red pepper. This makes more than you need for the oysters, but it will keep in the refrigerator. Use the oil when you want to add a little heat to a dish without the added vinegar found in hot sauce.

1 cup extra virgin olive oil
2^1/$_2$ teaspoons crushed red pepper flakes

Combine the olive oil and red pepper flakes in a small saucepan. Heat over medium heat until it starts to bubble lightly. Immediately remove from the heat and allow the red pepper flakes to steep in the olive oil until cool. Strain the oil and refrigerate it for up to a month.

SPICY GRILLED SHRIMP WITH GAZPACHO VINAIGRETTE SERVES 6

This is a great way to kick off a summer barbecue. The vinaigrette, which would also go well with grilled tuna or chicken, can be made a day ahead.

6 plum tomatoes, peeled, seeded, and finely diced

1 medium cucumber, preferably seedless, peeled and finely diced

1 red bell pepper, stemmed, seeded, and finely diced

1 jalapeño chile, stemmed, seeded, and finely diced

1/4 cup finely diced red onion

1/4 cup red wine vinegar

1/3 cup good-quality tomato juice

1/4 cup extra virgin olive oil, plus more if needed

Tabasco or other hot sauce

Kosher salt

1 1/2 pounds large shrimp (about 30), shelled and deveined

6 fresh basil leaves, cut into a chiffonade

Pinch of crushed red pepper flakes, or more to taste

Freshly ground black pepper

MAKE THE VINAIGRETTE In a small bowl, combine the tomatoes, cucumber, bell pepper, jalapeño, onion, vinegar, tomato juice, and 2 tablespoons of the olive oil. Season with a couple drops of Tabasco and a few good pinches of salt. Allow the mixture to sit at room temperature for at least an hour or refrigerate for up to a day to allow the flavors to meld. (If chilled, remove the vinaigrette from the refrigerator about half an hour before serving.)

MARINATE THE SHRIMP Toss the shrimp with the remaining 2 tablespoons of olive oil, the basil, and the red pepper flakes. Allow the shrimp to sit at room temperature for half an hour to soak up the flavors of the marinade or refrigerate the shrimp in the marinade for up to a day.

GRILL THE SHRIMP Heat the grill of your choice (or a grill pan if you are cooking indoors) to medium. Season the shrimp with salt and black pepper to taste. Grill the shrimp, brushing any extra marinade over them, until just barely cooked through, about 2 minutes on each side.

TO SERVE Taste the vinaigrette and season with additional salt, Tabasco, or vinegar if needed. Divide the vinaigrette among six small plates and set the warm shrimp on top. Serve immediately.

MIXED SEAFOOD STUFATO WITH SUNCHOKE AND CARAMELIZED SHALLOT PUREE SERVES 4

This is a pretty fussy dish but worth the effort for a special dinner. Many of the components can be made ahead and assembled just before serving. Also, you can play around with the combination of seafood, even leaving out the lobster and increasing the amounts of shrimp and mussels. I do, however, insist on the scallops; they go extremely well with the nutty, rich flavor of the sunchokes. I like the shrimp just barely heated by the puree; if you like shrimp more fully cooked, add them to the pan with the scallops for about 1 minute.

PUREE THE SUNCHOKES   In a medium pot, heat 2 tablespoons of the olive oil over medium heat. Add the shallots and cook until softened and well browned, about 10 minutes. Add the sunchokes and chicken broth and bring to a boil. Cook until the sunchokes are very soft, 15 to 20 minutes. Puree the mixture with a blender, adding another 2 tablespoons of the oil as you puree it. Strain the puree through a fine mesh strainer into a saucepan and reserve. (This can be made ahead and refrigerated for a day.)

MARINATE THE SHRIMP   In a small bowl, toss the shrimp with the rosemary, about 1 teaspoon of the garlic, a pinch of red pepper flakes, and about 1 ½ teaspoons of the olive oil. Allow to marinate for half an hour at room temperature or up to a day refrigerated. (Bring to room temperature before using.)

PARCOOK THE LOBSTER   Fill a pot large enough to hold the lobster with water and bring to a boil. Have ready a large bowl of ice water. Add the lobster head first and boil for 3 minutes to parcook the lobster (it will finish cooking in the hot puree). Plunge the lobster into the ice water to stop the cooking. Remove the meat from the tail and large claws and cut into bite-size chunks. Reserve. (You can cook the lobster up to a day ahead and refrigerate it. Bring to room temperature before using.)   *(continued)*

7 to 8 tablespoons extra virgin olive oil

2 shallots, thinly sliced

10 ounces sunchokes, peeled, trimmed, and roughly chopped

1 quart Chicken Broth (page 241)

4 extra-large shrimp or 3 Alaskan spot prawns, peeled, deveined, and chopped into bite-size pieces

1/4 teaspoon chopped fresh rosemary

3 garlic cloves, finely chopped

2 pinches of crushed red pepper flakes

1 lobster (about 1 1/4 pounds)

3 fresh thyme sprigs

1/2 pound (16 to 18) mussels, scrubbed and debearded

1/2 pound (6 to 8) littleneck clams

1/4 pound guanciale or pancetta, cut into 1/2-inch dice (1/2 cup)

4 sea scallops

Kosher salt and freshly ground black pepper

2 small potatoes, such as new potatoes, fingerlings, or purple Peruvian, diced and blanched

1 leek, white part only, diced and blanched

STEAM THE MUSSELS AND CLAMS   Heat 1 tablespoon of olive oil in a medium saucepan over medium heat. Add the remaining chopped garlic, a pinch of red pepper, and the thyme sprigs. Put the mussels and clams in the pan along with ¼ to ½ cup of water. Cover the pan and cook, increasing the heat if you want, until the clams and mussels open, 5 to 7 minutes. Drain in a colander set over a bowl to catch the liquid in the pan. Remove the meat from the shells and reserve it as well as the liquid. (The shellfish can be prepared earlier in the day and kept refrigerated. Bring to room temperature before using.)

CRISP THE GUANCIALE   Heat a small sauté pan, add the guanciale, and cook until it renders its fat and becomes crispy, 5 to 6 minutes. Reserve.

TO FINISH   Have ready four warmed soup bowls. Divide the shrimp and lobster among the four bowls. Heat the sunchoke puree over medium-high heat until hot but not boiling. Carefully add a little (2 to 4 tablespoons) of the reserved shellfish cooking liquid to the puree, leaving any sediment behind, to flavor it and thin it slightly.

Season the scallops with salt and pepper. In a separate sauté pan, heat 2 tablespoons of the olive oil over high heat. Add the scallops and brown them thoroughly on one side, 2 to 3 minutes. Turn the scallops and cook for another minute (2 minutes if the scallops are very large). Remove from the heat and let the residual heat from the pan finish cooking the scallops to medium rare.

Meanwhile, add the potatoes, leek, mussels, and clams to the hot puree to reheat them. Divide the puree among the four bowls. Slice the scallops in half and divide among the bowls. Sprinkle the guanciale over the top and serve immediately.

ROASTED MUSSELS SERVES 4

The secret to making mussels exceedingly full flavored is to cook them in chicken broth as well as wine, as I do in this otherwise classic rendition. In Italy, mussels—as well as all kinds of other dishes—are often cooked in wood-burning ovens, giving them a fabulous smoky flavor. If you have such an oven, you're very lucky, and I hope you use it a lot. Otherwise, cook the mussels in a regular oven as directed below; you don't get the smoky flavor, but the mussels cook tenderly and evenly. If you have a clay roaster, try cooking the mussels in that; it retains heat beautifully and can go from the oven to the table. Serve these with good crusty bread to mop up the sauce.

COOK THE MUSSELS Heat the oven to 300°F. In a large ovenproof pot or terra-cotta roaster with a lid, heat the olive oil over medium-low heat. Add the onion, garlic, and red pepper flakes and cook gently until tender but not colored, 10 minutes. Add the wine and broth and cook over medium-low heat for 15 minutes. Taste and season with a little salt, if necessary (you may not need any if your chicken broth is salty). Toss in the mussels, cover the pot, and cook in the oven until they open, 15 to 20 minutes.

TO SERVE Use a slotted spoon to transfer the mussels to four bowls or serve them right from the pot. If using serving bowls, pour the liquid from the pot over the mussels, leaving any sediment behind.

1 tablespoon extra virgin olive oil

1 medium onion, halved and very thinly sliced

2 garlic cloves, thinly sliced

$1/2$ teaspoon crushed red pepper flakes, or more to taste

1 cup dry white wine

1 cup Chicken Broth (page 241)

Kosher salt

3 to 4 pounds mussels, scrubbed and debearded

SALT-BAKED SHRIMP WITH
OLIVE OIL AND THYME SERVES 4 TO 6

While imparting just a bit of salty flavor, a salt bed cooks the shrimp at a consistent temperature without drying them out. The result: sweet, succulent shrimp that are plump and moist. Another advantage for entertaining is that the hot bed of salt will keep the shrimp warm for a while in a buffet.

MARINATE THE SHRIMP Toss together the shrimp, olive oil, thyme, and pepper to taste and marinate, refrigerated, for at least 20 minutes.

CREATE THE SALT BED AND BAKE Heat the oven to 350°F. In a bowl, stir the salt and egg whites together. Spread the salt over the bottom of a small sided baking sheet or a shallow baking dish about 9 by 13 inches; you need a depth of at least ½ inch. Remove the shrimp from the marinade and arrange them on the salt bed with a little space between each. Cook until pink and just cooked through, 12 to 15 minutes. Let the shrimp cool slightly, then let guests serve themselves from the pan.

24 large shrimp, unpeeled

3 tablespoons extra virgin olive oil

6 small fresh thyme sprigs

Freshly ground black pepper

1 pound kosher salt

2 large egg whites, lightly whisked

SEARED SCALLOPS WITH LEEKS, POTATO, AND SAUSAGE SERVES 4

Peppery leeks and earthy thyme temper the sweetness of sea scallops in this perfect-for-fall dish. I find scallops too rich to serve as a main course, but if you think otherwise, this would make a good meal for two. The only way to get beautifully browned scallops is to begin with "dry"—not chemically treated—ones; if not labeled as such ask the fishmonger.

2 tablespoons extra virgin olive oil, plus more if needed

2 to 3 leeks, white and light green parts, well washed and dried, cut into a medium dice (about 1 cup)

1 medium Yukon gold potato, peeled and diced (about 1 cup)

1 small fresh thyme sprig

Pinch of crushed red pepper flakes

1¹/₂ to 2 cups Chicken Broth (page 241)

¹/₄ pound sweet Italian sausage

8 large sea scallops

Kosher salt and freshly ground black pepper

1 tablespoon chopped fresh parsley

COOK THE VEGETABLES Heat the oven to 400°F. Heat 1½ tablespoons of the olive oil over medium-high heat in an ovenproof sauté pan. Add the leeks and cook until lightly browned, about 10 minutes. Add the potato, thyme, red pepper flakes, and 1½ cups chicken broth. Transfer the pan to the oven and cook, uncovered, until the potatoes are cooked through and the leeks are meltingly tender, 45 minutes to an hour. Check on the vegetables about halfway through cooking; the broth will reduce somewhat, allowing the potatoes to brown slightly, which is fine. If the pan gets too dry (you'll want a little liquid in the final dish), add a little more broth. When the vegetables are cooked, remove them from the oven but keep them warm in the pan.

CRISP THE SAUSAGE Meanwhile, heat a small sauté pan over medium-high heat. Remove the sausage from its casing and put it in the pan. (You may need to add a little olive oil if your sausage is very lean.) As it browns, break it into little pieces with a wooden spoon. When the sausage is cooked through and well browned, remove the pan from the heat.

SEAR THE SCALLOPS   Season the scallops well with salt and pepper. Heat a couple teaspoons of olive oil in a sauté pan over high heat. Add the scallops and brown well on one side for 2 to 3 minutes. Turn the scallops and cook for another minute (2 minutes if the scallops are very large). Remove from the heat but leave the scallops in the hot pan for another minute or two to finish cooking.

TO SERVE   Reheat the sausage over high heat. Spoon the potatoes and leeks, along with some of the broth, on rimmed serving plates. Put the scallops on top of the vegetables and top with the crisped, crumbled sausage. Finish with a sprinkle of parsley and serve immediately.

RAW SHELLFISH WITH CUCUMBER AND TOMATO SALAD   SERVES 4

Cucumbers and raw shellfish are a natural match; the cucumber extends the flavor of the clams and adds a refreshing crunch.

3/4 cup peeled, shredded cucumber

1/4 cup seeded, finely diced tomato

1/4 teaspoon finely chopped fresh chives

1 teaspoon red wine vinegar, or more to taste

Kosher salt and freshly ground black pepper

16 razor clams or 8 dry, diver-caught sea scallops, thinly sliced

Pinch of sea salt

1 cup mixed micro or baby greens, well washed and dried

In a small bowl, combine the cucumber, tomato, chives, and vinegar. Mix gently, seasoning lightly with salt and just a touch of pepper. Divide the clams among four chilled serving plates, fanning them out. Mound a spoonful of the cucumber mixture next to the clams. Top each plate with a tiny sprinkle of sea salt and a garnish of greens.

LEMON AND GARLIC SARDINES WITH ARTICHOKE "PANZANELLA" SERVES 4

Unlike classic panzanella, an Italian bread salad made with soaked, softened bread, this version uses croutons, which give the salad a welcome crunch. If you love sardines and want even more of this strong fish flavor, drizzle some of the cooking oil from the sardines over the finished dish. Some lightly dressed baby greens would go well on the side, too.

COOK THE SARDINES   In a small saucepan, combine the olive oil, garlic, lemon and lime zest, thyme, and red pepper flakes and heat over low heat until the garlic starts to sizzle, about 5 minutes. Add the sardines and cook for 2 minutes. Take the pan off the heat and let the sardines poach in the oil for at least 30 minutes. Check a sardine to see if it's cooked through (it will be opaque in its center; if not, re-heat briefly in the oil until cooked through).

MAKE THE PANZANELLA   Cut the lemon in half. Squeeze one half into a small bowl of water. Trim the artichokes and remove the chokes. Slice the hearts thinly and put them in the lemon water to prevent browning. Squeeze the remaining lemon half into another small bowl. Add about 2 tablespoons of olive oil and season lightly with kosher salt.

Heat a medium sauté pan over medium heat. Add the remaining 2 tablespoons of olive oil. When hot, add the bread cubes and cook, tossing, until evenly browned and crisp, adding more oil as needed. Using a slotted spoon, transfer to a small bowl. Remove the artichokes from the acidulated water and add them as well as the mint to the bread; toss well.

TO SERVE   Divide the panzanella among four small plates. Drizzle each with about 2 teaspoons of the lemon and olive oil mixture. Lay the sardines across the top and serve with a little sea salt sprinkled on top.

FOR THE SARDINES

1 cup extra virgin olive oil

2 garlic cloves, cut in half

Strips of zest from 1/2 lemon

Strips of zest from 1/2 lime

3 fresh thyme sprigs

1/2 to 1 teaspoon crushed red pepper flakes

8 fresh sardine fillets (7 to 8 ounces)

FOR THE PANZANELLA

1 lemon (use the zested one from the sardines)

2 artichokes

1/4 cup extra virgin olive oil, plus more if needed

Kosher salt

1 cup 1/4-inch cubes Italian bread

1 teaspoon chopped fresh mint

Sea salt

Light Salads and Soups

The salads here are intended to be served as either the beginning or the end of a meal. (You'll find main-course salads in the next chapter.) I love green, leafy salads, but also enjoy serving salads composed of artichokes, cucumbers, and other vegetables. With salads, even more than in cooked dishes, all ingredients must be premium. If the greens you had in mind look tired and past their prime, choose others that are similar in character, whether mild like Bibb and red leaf lettuce, or more bitter and peppery, such as arugula, watercress, and radicchio.

I have been on a soup kick lately and am especially fond of pureed soups. Instead of using cream to make my avocado, asparagus, or cauliflower rich and smooth, I add ample olive oil. Because I'm not overloading the soup with buttery fat, the intense flavor of the puree itself always shines through. I will often use the same base puree, say a fresh pea soup, and toy with it to create very different final flavors that appear on my menu over the course of the month or season. I love how adding even a single ingredient—tarragon, for example—can change the entire character of the soup. I also strive to come up with exciting, complementary accompaniments to my soups, which is especially important with purees. Without some contrasting texture and additional flavorings, every spoonful of a pureed soup will taste the same, which quickly becomes boring—something I strive never to be.

I create my soups assuming they will be served as a first course, and tailor portions accordingly. The heartier ones—Clam and Potato Soup with Wilted Greens and Crispy Bacon (page 51) and Chickpea Soup with Sausage, Cabbage, and Rosemary (page 58)—would make an excellent lunch or light dinner in larger portions.

MIXED GREENS WITH MARINATED CHERRY TOMATOES AND SHALLOTS SERVES 6

As with most of my salads, I like to "hide" the main ingredients under the leafy greens. The main reason I do this is to avoid crushing delicate greens under the heavier components of the salad. The fringe benefit is the bit of surprise that comes with eating a salad assembled this way: "Oh, *there* are the tomatoes!"

1 pint cherry tomatoes, cut in half

1/2 cup plus 1 1/2 tablespoons extra virgin olive oil

1 1/2 tablespoons red wine vinegar

3 tablespoons balsamic vinegar

1 1/2 teaspoons finely chopped fresh oregano

1 1/2 teaspoons finely chopped fresh basil

Kosher salt and freshly ground black pepper

1 teaspoon Dijon mustard

6 handfuls of your favorite mixed greens (8 to 10 ounces), well washed and dried

Marinated Shallots (page 67)

1 ounce Parmigiano-Reggiano

MARINATE THE TOMATOES   Combine the tomatoes with the 1½ tablespoons of olive oil, 1½ teaspoons of the red wine vinegar, 1 tablespoon of the balsamic vinegar, the oregano, the basil, and a couple pinches of salt. Let sit at room temperature for 30 minutes to an hour to meld the flavors. (You can also refrigerate the tomatoes for up to 8 hours, but let them sit at room temperature before assembling the salad.)

WHISK THE VINAIGRETTE   In a small bowl, whisk together the remaining 1 tablespoon of red wine vinegar, 2 tablespoons of balsamic vinegar, ½ cup of olive oil, and the mustard. Season to taste with salt and pepper.

TO SERVE   Toss the greens with just enough of the vinaigrette to coat lightly. Divide the tomatoes among six serving plates. Mound the greens over the tomatoes and sprinkle the shallots over the greens (leave the marinating liquid behind). Top with shavings of Parmigiano and serve.

HERBED GOAT CHEESE AND RAMP SALAD SERVES 4

If you've ever seen ramps—wild onions that resemble scallions but with a broader leaf—at a farmers' market and wondered what the hell to do with them, the answer is here in this lovely and simple salad. The dressing for the greens contains a lot of vinegar, but the olive oil used in cooking the ramps, plus the oil baked with the cheese, rounds out the flavor.

Heat the oven to 300°F.

FLAVOR THE GOAT CHEESE Combine the goat cheese and the basil and mash them together well with a fork. Season to taste with salt and pepper.

SAUTÉ THE RAMPS In a medium sauté pan, heat 3 tablespoons of the olive oil over medium heat. Add the ramps, season with a little salt (if you have sea salt, even better), and cook, stirring occasionally, until the ramps are tender, about 7 minutes. Add 1 tablespoon of the vinegar, toss, and take off the heat.

TO SERVE Using a tablespoon, divide the goat cheese into four rounds and put them in a small baking dish. Drizzle about 2 tablespoons of olive oil over the goat cheese and bake until the cheese begins to melt, about 5 minutes. Meanwhile, combine the remaining 3 tablespoons olive oil with 4 tablespoons vinegar and lightly dress the greens (you may not need all of the vinaigrette). Divide the ramps among four plates. Top with the warmed goat cheese and the greens, season with salt and pepper, and serve.

4 ounces fresh goat cheese

6 fresh basil leaves, finely chopped

Kosher salt and freshly ground black pepper

1/2 cup extra virgin olive oil

16 thin ramps, roots trimmed and leaves washed

5 tablespoons sherry vinegar

2 handfuls mixed baby greens (about 3 ounces), well washed and dried

GRILLED EGGPLANT, MARINATED TOMATO, AND ARUGULA SALAD SERVES 4

I don't seed the tomatoes for this salad because I like the flavor and additional texture the seeds provide.

$3/4$ cup extra virgin olive oil, plus more for grilling the eggplant

2 tablespoons red wine vinegar

2 tablespoons balsamic vinegar

$1^1/2$ teaspoons chopped fresh oregano

4 basil leaves, cut into a chiffonade

Kosher salt and freshly ground black pepper

8 plum tomatoes, peeled and cut into $3/4$-inch pieces

1 large or 2 medium Italian eggplants (about $1^1/2$ pounds), peeled and sliced lengthwise $1/8$ inch thick

1 teaspoon Dijon mustard

2 small bunches arugula, well washed, dried, and any tough stems removed

1 ounce grana Padano or Parmigiano-Reggiano

MARINATE THE TOMATOES   In a medium bowl, whisk together ¼ cup of the olive oil, 1 tablespoon of the red wine vinegar, 1 tablespoon of the balsamic vinegar, the oregano, and the basil. Season with salt and pepper. Add the tomatoes and toss to coat. Let stand at room temperature at least 45 minutes or up to 24 hours refrigerated.

SALT THE EGGPLANT   Put the eggplant slices in a colander and toss with 1 teaspoon of kosher salt. Put the colander in a clean sink, weight the eggplant, and allow the salt to draw out the excess moisture for 30 minutes.

GRILL THE EGGPLANT   Heat an outdoor grill or a grill pan to medium-high heat. Pat the eggplant slices dry and brush both sides with olive oil. Grill for a couple of minutes on both sides; you want the eggplant to brown lightly and get just barely crisp around the edges. Cool in a single layer, preferably on a cooling rack, so the eggplant doesn't steam and become mushy.

DRESS THE GREENS In a small bowl, whisk together the remaining ½ cup of olive oil, 1 tablespoon of red wine vinegar, 1 tablespoon of balsamic vinegar, and the mustard. Season with salt and pepper. Very lightly dress the arugula with some of this vinaigrette just before assembling the salad.

TO SERVE Divide the tomatoes among four large plates. Lay strips of eggplant on a cutting board, overlapping them slightly to form a rectangle measuring about 7 by 5 inches. Lay a handful of the dressed arugula along the bottom edge of the rectangle and roll the eggplant up around the arugula, allowing some of the greens to peek out at both ends. Repeat with more eggplant and arugula until you have four rolls. Either lay one whole roll on each plate or slice each roll in half crosswise and position the halves on top of the tomatoes with their cut side down, two halves per plate. Shave some grana Padano over the top.

ROASTED BABY BEET SALAD WITH ROBIOLA CHEESE AND BANYULS VINAIGRETTE SERVES 4

A mix of different-colored beets makes this a stunning salad, but it will taste just as good with a single color, or with larger beets cut into pieces. Roasting beets on salt helps them keep their shape while cooking. Aromatic and mellow, Banyuls vinegar is made from a fortified wine of the same name. If you can't find it, substitute a good-quality red wine vinegar or a Port vinegar, preferably one that's not too acidic. Be careful when handling the beets and the reduction as the color will stain not only clothes but potentially your work surface, too. To avoid this, cut them on an old (clean) towel or a stack of paper towels and consider wearing rubber gloves when handling beets if you don't want pink fingertips.

ROAST THE BEETS   Heat the oven to 450°F. Pour kosher salt into a 9 by 13-inch baking pan to a depth of ½ inch. Put the beets on top of the salt, wrap the pan in foil, and roast until tender (a paring knife inserted will pull out easily), about 45 minutes (longer for larger beets). When the beets are cool enough to handle, peel them and cut in half if small or into wedges if large. (The beets can be roasted a day or two ahead of serving.)

MAKE THE VINAIGRETTE   Combine the vinegar and olive oil. Season to taste with salt.

TO SERVE   Heat the oven to 300°F. Put the beets on a baking sheet, drizzle them with a little oil, and sprinkle the chopped almonds on top. Heat until warmed, 3 to 6 minutes.

In a bowl, combine the greens, frisée, and endive and toss with enough vinaigrette to coat them well. Divide the warm beets among four plates. Scatter the cheese around and over the beets. Top with the greens mixture and serve.

1 pound or more kosher salt for roasting the beets, plus more for seasoning

12 to 16 baby beets, preferably a mix of colors, well washed, stems and roots trimmed

¼ cup Banyuls vinegar, Port vinegar, or red wine vinegar

¾ cup extra virgin olive oil, plus more for drizzling

½ cup sliced almonds, toasted and chopped

2 small handfuls mixed baby greens (about 3 ounces), well washed and dried

1 small head frisée, outer leaves and tough core removed, remaining leaves separated, well washed and dried

12 endive leaves, from about 1 head (a mix of red and white leaves is especially pretty if you don't mind the leftovers)

½ pound Robiola or other creamy cheese, such as Camembert or Taleggio, cut into bite-size pieces

In this salad, I leave the greens undressed to allow the subtle, nutty flavor of the artichokes to come through.

SLICED ARTICHOKE SALAD SERVES 4

Allowing the artichokes to soak for a while in acidulated water is the key to serving them raw without undue bitterness.

6 lemons, cut in half

6 medium artichokes, trimmed down to the heart, chokes removed

4 handfuls mixed baby greens (about 6 ounces), well washed and dried

3 tablespoons extra virgin olive oil

Kosher salt and freshly ground black pepper

2 ounces Parmigiano-Reggiano

SOAK THE ARTICHOKES Squeeze the juice from 5 of the lemons into a small bowl. (Reserve the other lemon for serving.) Slice the artichokes very thinly, preferably with a mandoline, adding them to the lemon juice as you slice. Add enough water to keep the artichokes completely covered in liquid (weight them down to keep them under). Let them soak for at least 1½ hours and preferably overnight.

ASSEMBLE THE SALAD Remove the artichokes from the water and pat dry. Divide the greens among four salad plates and top with the artichokes. Drizzle olive oil over each plate and spritz with the remaining lemon. Season with salt and pepper. Use a vegetable peeler to shave the Parmigiano over the artichokes.

MARINATED CUCUMBER SALAD WITH RICOTTA SALATA   SERVES 4

Crisp and refreshing, this salad would be especially welcome following a rich appetizer. If you want to add a crunchy texture, sprinkle a few crisp croutons on each plate.

3/4 cup extra virgin olive oil

3 tablespoons white wine vinegar

12 fresh basil leaves, torn

Pinch of crushed red pepper flakes

Kosher salt

2 cucumbers, peeled and thinly sliced

1 tablespoon red wine vinegar

2 tablespoons balsamic vinegar

Freshly ground black pepper

2 handfuls mixed baby greens (about 3 ounces), well washed and dried

1/2 cup grated ricotta salata or crumbled feta cheese

MARINATE THE CUCUMBERS   In a medium bowl, whisk together 1/4 cup of the olive oil, the white wine vinegar, the basil, the red pepper flakes, and 1/2 teaspoon salt. Add the cucumbers, toss to combine, and let sit, at room temperature or refrigerated, for 2 to 3 hours.

WHISK THE VINAIGRETTE   In a small bowl, whisk together the red wine vinegar, balsamic vinegar, and remaining 1/2 cup of olive oil. Season to taste with salt and pepper.

TO SERVE   Divide the cucumbers among four serving plates. Toss the greens with just enough vinaigrette to lightly coat the leaves. Mound the greens over the cucumbers and sprinkle the cheese on top.

ASPARAGUS SOUP WITH MUSSELS SERVES 4

Mussels and asparagus may not be a classic food match, but the combination really works well in this soup. If you want an immediate visual clue that there are mussels in the puree, leave a couple in their shells and garnish the soup with them. I love this; it's my favorite springtime soup.

MAKE THE ASPARAGUS PUREE Chop the asparagus into ½-inch pieces, reserving about half of the tips separately. Heat 1 tablespoon of the olive oil in a saucepan over medium-high heat. Add the shallots, red pepper flakes, and a large pinch of salt. Cook, stirring occasionally, until the shallots are tender and just taking on some color, about 5 minutes. Add the asparagus (but not the reserved tips) and cook for about 1 minute. Add the broth plus 1 cup of water and bring to a boil, then reduce the heat to a robust simmer and cook until the asparagus is tender. Let cool a bit and then puree the soup in batches, adding 1½ tablespoons of olive oil as you puree it. Return the soup to a clean saucepan, season to taste with salt, and reserve. (The puree can be made ahead and refrigerated for a day.)

STEAM THE MUSSELS Heat 1 tablespoon of olive oil in a large saucepan over high heat. Add the mussels and ½ cup of water and cover. Cook until almost all of the mussels have opened wide, 3 to 5 minutes. Remove the mussels from the pot. Pour the liquid into a measuring cup, being careful to leave any grit behind. When the mussels are cool enough to handle, remove them from their shells.

TO FINISH Heat a teaspoon of olive oil in a small sauté pan over medium-high heat and sauté the carrots just until lightly colored. Add the reserved mussel cooking liquid to the asparagus puree and reheat over medium-low heat. Add the leek, peas, carrots, and asparagus tips and cook until the vegetables are crisp-tender, about 5 minutes. Add the mussels and the chives and cook just until heated through. Serve immediately in warm soup bowls.

1 pound asparagus, tough ends trimmed

About 4 tablespoons extra virgin olive oil

2 medium shallots, sliced lengthwise into thin slivers (about $^1/_3$ cup)

Pinch of crushed red pepper flakes

Kosher salt

2 cups Chicken Broth (page 241)

$1^1/_2$ pounds mussels, scrubbed and debearded

$^1/_2$ cup finely diced carrots

1 leek, white and light green parts, cut into a medium dice and rinsed well

1 cup fresh or frozen peas

1 teaspoon chopped fresh chives

CLAM AND POTATO SOUP WITH WILTED GREENS AND CRISPY BACON SERVES 4 TO 6

I grew up in New England (Connecticut), and my grandparents had a potato farm in Maine. In other words, I have eaten clam chowder all my life. My version riffs on the classic while maintaining the integrity of why people like chowder in the first place, with ample olive oil taking the place of the cream to give this soup its unctuous texture. (Just don't pour a very fruity olive oil or it will overwhelm the clam flavor.) Using skin-on new potatoes or purple Peruvians gives the soup some really nice additional color but you could use all Yukon gold.

PREPARE THE CLAMS   Rinse the clams well. Heat about 1 tablespoon of the olive oil in a large saucepan over medium heat. Add the garlic and cook, stirring occasionally, until golden and fragrant. Add the thyme and red pepper flakes. Add the clams and 1 cup of the chicken broth. Cover the pot and steam until the clams open, about 5 minutes. Transfer the open clams to a large bowl. Strain the cooking liquid into a 1-quart measuring cup, leaving any sediment behind.

Working over a bowl, remove the clam meat from the shell. Add any more collected juices to the measuring cup with the clam cooking liquid; you should have about ¾ cup. Reserve the clam meat. (This can be done a day ahead; refrigerate the clam broth and the meat separately.)

MAKE THE POTATO PUREE   Heat 2 tablespoons of the olive oil in a large saucepan over medium heat. Add the shallot and rosemary and cook until the shallot is soft, about 5 minutes. Meanwhile, add enough chicken broth to the reserved clam cooking liquid to equal 1 quart. Add the Yukon gold potatoes and this broth to the saucepan. Increase the heat and bring to a boil, then reduce to a simmer and cook until the potatoes are very tender, about 15 minutes. Remove the rosemary and discard. Either right in the pot with a hand

1½ pounds littleneck clams

6 tablespoons extra virgin olive oil, plus more if needed

1 garlic clove, chopped

1 small fresh thyme sprig

Pinch of crushed red pepper flakes

1 quart Chicken Broth (page 241)

1 shallot, thinly sliced

1 small fresh rosemary sprig

2 pounds Yukon gold potatoes, peeled and cut into a large dice

Kosher salt and freshly ground black pepper

2 small new potatoes or purple Peruvians, cut into a small dice (about ¾ cup)

2 ounces bacon, diced

6 ounces dandelion or other bitter greens, tough stems removed, well washed and dried

blender or in a food processor or blender in batches, puree the soup, adding another 2 to 3 tablespoons olive oil as you go. Season to taste with salt and pepper. (The puree can be made a day ahead and refrigerated.)

TO FINISH   Boil the new potatoes in well-salted water until just tender. In a medium sauté pan, cook the bacon until crispy, adding a little olive oil if needed. Remove the bacon from the pan, but don't wash the pan. Add the greens to the pan and cook, tossing occasionally, until just barely wilted and still bright green, about 2 minutes. (The water from washing the greens should provide enough liquid, but more water can be added if the pan becomes too dry.) Add the clams and cook, stirring occasionally, until warmed through. Reheat the puree, if necessary. Divide the clams, greens, and potatoes among large warm soup bowls. Divide the puree among the bowls and top each with some crisped bacon.

ALMOND GAZPACHO SERVES 4

This cold, vibrant soup launches a hot summer night's meal perfectly, and you can make it almost instantly. The garnish list, while it looks long, pulls together quickly when you're serving only four people, composed as it is of just a few grapes to peel and a small bit of apple to slice. (Of course, that's not the case when I serve this in volume at the restaurant, but that's my problem, not yours.)

MAKE THE SOUP   In a food processor or blender, grind the 1 cup of almonds, the garlic, and a pinch of salt until finely ground. With the motor running, add the vinegar and 5 tablespoons of the olive oil. Stop the motor, scrape down the sides, and add the broth. Blend for a few minutes to combine well. Strain the soup through a fine mesh strainer, pushing on the solids to make sure that all of the almond flavor transfers. Chill the soup for at least 1 hour.

TO SERVE   Taste the cold soup and season with salt and additional vinegar if necessary. Divide the soup among four bowls. In a small bowl, using your fingers, lightly combine the 1 tablespoon of slivered almonds, apple, grapes, and scallop, if using. Divide the mixture among the four bowls. Finish each bowl with a tiny drizzle of olive oil, a squeeze of lemon juice, and a tiny pinch of paprika.

1 cup plus 1 tablespoon slivered almonds

1 small garlic clove, blanched

Kosher salt

2 tablespoons red wine vinegar, or more to taste

6 tablespoons extra virgin olive oil

3 cups chicken or vegetable broth

1 tablespoon slivered apple

1 tablespoon peeled, slivered grapes

1 raw scallop, diced (optional)

$1^{1}/_{2}$ teaspoons fresh lemon juice

Pinch of smoked paprika (also called *pimentón*)

CAULIFLOWER SOUP WITH OYSTERS SERVES 6

Because the oysters get cooked by the hot soup, it would be okay to buy previously shucked oysters, but the best flavor will come from freshly shucked ones. Some fishmongers will do the shucking for you, but be very careful transporting them as you need the oyster juice for the soup. For an even more exciting soup, add a little of the Caper Salmoriglio. Its briny, salty flavor contrasts with the earthiness of the cauliflower while complementing the oysters.

1 medium head cauliflower (about 2 pounds)

2 tablespoons extra virgin olive oil

1 small onion, chopped

$1/4$ teaspoon crushed red pepper flakes, or more to taste

2 cups whole milk

2 cups Chicken Broth (page 241)

18 raw oysters plus their juice

$1^1/2$ teaspoons minced fresh chives

Caper Salmoriglio (page 133; optional)

MAKE THE CAULIFLOWER PUREE   Trim the cauliflower and chop it; reserve ½ cup of tiny (about ¼ inch) florets as a garnish. Heat a tablespoon of the olive oil over medium heat. Add the onion and red pepper flakes and cook, stirring often, until the onion is tender, about 7 minutes. Add the cauliflower, milk, and chicken broth and cook, uncovered, until the cauliflower is very tender, 15 to 20 minutes. Puree the soup well in a blender. (You can make the soup a day ahead and refrigerate it, covered; also refrigerate the reserved cauliflower florets.)

TO SERVE   Shuck the oysters and pour their juice into a small bowl. Strain the juice into a small measuring cup. Bring the soup to a gentle boil. Put 3 oysters in each of six warm soup bowls. Add about a tablespoon of the oyster juice to each bowl. Divide the reserved cauliflower florets among the bowls, too. Pour the hot soup over the oysters and florets, top with the chives, and serve immediately, drizzled with a small amount of Caper Salmoriglio if you like.

AVOCADO SOUP WITH SHRIMP SERVES 4

This cool soup, while not exactly Italian, is perfect on a hot summer day. The shrimp are served *crudo* style, but if raw fish is not your thing, you can sear the shrimp or leave them out altogether, substituting, say, some chopped yellow tomatoes instead.

MARINATE THE SHRIMP   Cut each shrimp into 6 pieces. In a small bowl, toss the shrimp with the onion, 1½ tablespoons of the olive oil, and the chives. Refrigerate for a couple of hours or up to one day.

MAKE THE SOUP   Combine the avocados, milk, and broth and puree in a blender until smooth, adding a little more broth if very thick. Season with salt and pepper and chill for at least 2 hours and up to a day before serving.

MAKE THE CROUTONS   Heat the remaining ½ tablespoon of olive oil in a small sauté pan over medium-high heat. Add the bread cubes, reduce the heat to medium, and cook, turning the bread with tongs, until lightly browned on all sides. Remove from the pan and drain on a paper towel.

TO SERVE   Divide the shrimp among four bowls. Taste the soup and season again with salt and pepper if need be, as chilling can dull flavor. Divide the soup among the bowls, top with the croutons, and serve.

8 large shrimp, shelled and deveined

2 tablespoons finely chopped red onion

2 tablespoons extra virgin olive oil

1½ teaspoons chopped fresh chives

4 very ripe avocados

1 cup whole milk

1 cup Chicken Broth (page 241), plus more if needed

Kosher salt and freshly ground black pepper

1 slice Italian or country-style bread, cubed

CRANBERRY BEAN SOUP WITH ROSEMARY AND PANCETTA SERVES 6 TO 8

Cranberry, or borlotti, beans are kidney shaped with red streaks. Used in all kinds of Italian soups and stews, they're worth seeking. If you can't find them, substitute navy or cannellini beans. If you like a little heat, go for the larger amount of pepper flakes. This soup is pure comfort.

1 pound dried cranberry beans

4 to 5 tablespoons extra virgin olive oil

1 medium onion, chopped

2 garlic cloves, chopped

2 small rosemary sprigs

2-ounce chunk of pancetta

$^1/_4$ to $^1/_2$ teaspoon crushed red pepper flakes

3 quarts Chicken Broth (page 241)

Kosher salt and freshly ground black pepper

SOAK THE BEANS   Soak the beans in water to cover for at least 8 hours.

MAKE THE SOUP   Heat 2 tablespoons of the olive oil in a soup pot over medium heat. Add the onion and cook, stirring occasionally, until just tender, about 7 minutes. Add the garlic, rosemary, pancetta, and red pepper flakes and cook, stirring, another 2 to 3 minutes. Drain the beans and add them to the pot along with the chicken broth. Bring to a boil, then lower to a simmer and cook, uncovered, until the beans are pleasantly tender, about 1 hour (sometimes longer, depending on the beans); taste a bean to determine tenderness.

With a slotted spoon, remove the soup's solids to a large, sided baking sheet; this will make it easier to find the rosemary and pancetta. Discard the rosemary. When the pancetta is cool enough, cut it into a small dice. Set aside about a quarter of the beans in a bowl and toss them with the pancetta. Puree the remaining beans along with the broth either in the pot with a handheld immersion blender or in batches in a food processor or blender. As you puree, add 2 to 3 tablespoons of olive oil, a little at a time, to create a creamy, emulsified soup.

TO SERVE   Reheat the soup briefly, adding the reserved beans and pancetta; add more broth to thin the soup if you like. Season with pepper and—if needed—salt, and serve.

CHILLED PEA SOUP WITH CRAB, RIESLING, AND TARRAGON SERVES 4

Sweet Riesling adds a crisp, lively freshness. Although I'm a stickler about being sure wine is cooked off for most recipes, in this case I actually want wine added to the soup at the end so its essence really shines. Exactly how much to add will depend on your specific wine and your palate, so I suggest a range.

MAKE THE SOUP   In a medium saucepan, heat 1 tablespoon of the olive oil over medium heat. Add the shallots, season with a generous pinch of salt, and cook until tender, about 5 minutes. Reserve ¼ cup of the peas. Add the rest to the pot along with the chicken broth. Increase the heat to medium-high and cook the peas until tender, 2 to 3 minutes. Add the tarragon, transfer the mixture to a blender or food processor (or use a hand blender right in the pot), and puree it, adding 1 tablespoon of olive oil as you do so. Refrigerate the soup.

TO SERVE   In a small bowl, whisk together the remaining 2 tablespoons of olive oil and the lemon juice. Add the crab, tomatoes, and chives and toss gently. Season to taste with salt and pepper. Stir ½ cup of the Riesling into the soup. Taste and add more wine if you like and more salt if needed. Divide the soup among serving bowls and top with a spoonful of the crab mixture.

^{1}/4 cup extra virgin olive oil

3 shallots, thinly sliced

Kosher salt

1 pound shelled fresh or frozen peas (about 4 cups)

2 cups Chicken Broth (page 241)

1 tablespoon chopped fresh tarragon

2 teaspoons fresh lemon juice

^{1}/2 pound fresh lump crabmeat, picked over for shells

2 plum tomatoes, peeled and diced

2 teaspoons chopped fresh chives

Freshly ground black pepper

^{1}/2 cup to 1 cup sweet Riesling

CHICKPEA SOUP WITH SAUSAGE, CABBAGE, AND ROSEMARY   SERVES 6 TO 8

Though canned chickpeas are fine when used raw, I find that when cooked the flavor is very offputting. Starting with dried *ceci* (the Italian word for chickpea) takes more time but gives the soup a wonderfully earthy flavor.

1 pound dried chickpeas (about 2^1/4 cups)

^{1}/2 cup extra virgin olive oil

1 large onion, thinly sliced

1 fresh rosemary sprig, plus 1 tablespoon chopped

1 teaspoon kosher salt, plus more for seasoning

Freshly ground black pepper

2 ounces pancetta, chopped

1 shallot, chopped

4 ounces Napa cabbage, cut into 1-inch pieces

^{1}/2 pound sweet Italian sausage, removed from the casing and crumbled

1 to 2 cups Chicken Broth (page 241), as needed

1 plum tomato, peeled, seeded, and diced

1 tablespoon chopped fresh parsley

MAKE THE CHICKPEA PUREE   Soak the chickpeas overnight in enough water to cover well. In a large pot, heat 2 tablespoons of the olive oil over medium heat and cook the onion, stirring occasionally, until lightly browned, 10 to 12 minutes. Drain the chickpeas and put them in the pot. Add the rosemary sprig and enough fresh water to cover the chickpeas by at least 3 inches, about 12 cups. Bring the water to a boil and then lower to a simmer, cover, and cook the beans until they are extremely tender, about 1 hour, adding more water as necessary so the beans are always completely covered. Toward the end of cooking time, add the teaspoon of salt. When done, drain the beans, reserving the cooking liquid. Allow the beans to cool off a bit.

Set aside half of the cooked chickpeas. Discard the rosemary sprig. Puree the rest of the beans with some of the cooking liquid, in batches if necessary, until you have a creamy mixture that can coat the back of a ladle. As you puree, add 1½ tablespoons of olive oil, being sure it's well blended into the soup. Season to taste with salt and pepper and then strain the soup through a fine mesh strainer into a clean saucepan. (The puree can be made a day ahead and refrigerated.)

COOK THE PANCETTA AND CABBAGE   In a small saucepan, heat 1 tablespoon of the olive oil over medium-high heat. Add the pancetta and cook until lightly browned, about 5 minutes. Add another tablespoon of olive oil, the shallot, and the cabbage and cook until lightly browned, another 5 to 6 minutes. Add the reserved chickpeas, remove from heat, and set aside.

COOK THE SAUSAGE   In a sauté pan, heat the remaining olive oil over medium-high heat. Add the sausage and cook until well browned. Remove the sausage, leaving the oil in the pan. Drain the sausage on paper towels to draw out excess oil. Heat the chopped rosemary in the reserved oil over medium heat for a couple of minutes to infuse its flavor.

TO SERVE   Have warm soup bowls ready. Add the sausage to the cabbage and chickpeas and reheat. Reheat the chickpea puree, adding chicken broth if it's too thick. Just before serving, add the tomato to the sausage and chickpeas and divide the mixture among the soup bowls. Pour the hot puree over, drizzle with the reserved rosemary oil, and sprinkle with the parsley.

This is a very hearty soup, perfect for fall.

Eggs, Panini, and Hearty Salads

These recipes are sort of "anything goes" in that you can use them in different ways. For instance, I have served a version of the Shirred Eggs in Spinach Puree (page 62) as a very glamorous starter using a one-hour poached quail egg and adorning the dish with guanciale and fresh truffles. The somewhat pared-down version here, while it would make an excellent appetizer, would also be glorious as a special breakfast. The Potato Gatto (page 63), my latest "I could eat this every day" favorite, is a giant mashed potato cake bound with egg yolks, lightened with egg whites, and filled with all kinds of goodness—ham, salami, mozzarella. This you can eat as an appetizer, main course, or side dish. Italians will eat *gatto di patate* as the main dish for dinner and then serve leftovers the next night alongside a piece of meat. From my own experience I know it works any time of the day, from breakfast right on through to the best midnight snack. (In fact, there have been days when *gatto* is all I have eaten through the day.)

Finally, we have panini. I once oversaw a bar that served these almost exclusively. Everybody who ate there was happy. But I have also seen far too many horrible panini around town. Yes, a panini is "just" a sandwich, but if you want it to be good, you have to start with the best ingredients (excellent bread, quality meats, the best cheese) and then use them sparingly. A panini is as much about the perfectly crisped bread as about what's inside. Once you try the two I've included here, go ahead and get creative using your own favorite fillings. While panini served with a light salad make a great lunch, they can also be cut into small pieces and served as an hors d'oeuvre. And, as you can see by turning to page 211, you can even serve panini for dessert.

SHIRRED EGGS IN SPINACH PUREE SERVES 6

A perfectly cooked egg nestled in a beautiful spinach puree scented with truffle oil is some sensuous stuff. If you don't serve this with some grilled or toasted bread, however, your guests will love you less. This also makes an awesome breakfast; if serving that way, go ahead and crack two eggs per serving into the puree.

1 tablespoon extra virgin olive oil

1/4 cup thinly sliced shallot (about 1 large)

Kosher salt

10 ounces spinach, well washed, tough stems removed, and coarsely chopped

1 cup Chicken Broth (page 241)

2 teaspoons white truffle oil

6 large eggs

Freshly ground black pepper

MAKE THE PUREE   In a medium saucepan, heat the olive oil over medium heat. Add the shallot and a pinch of salt and cook, stirring until tender and lightly browned, about 5 minutes. Add the spinach, season with a pinch more salt, and cook, tossing until wilted and most of the released liquid has cooked off. Add the broth and bring to a boil. Take the spinach off the heat and let cool a little. Puree it well using a handheld or regular blender. The puree can be made a day ahead. Cover and refrigerate until ready to use.

COOK THE EGGS   Heat the oven to 300°F. If you've chilled the spinach puree, take it out of the refrigerator to let it warm up at room temperature. Stir in the truffle oil, taste, and add more salt if needed.

Put six ramekins (I use a 4-ounce size) on a baking sheet. Divide the puree among the ramekins, crack an egg into each, and bake until the eggs are just barely set. Start checking at 12 minutes, but this can take as long as 20 minutes. The time will vary depending on the size of your ramekins, the size of your eggs, and the temperature your ingredients were at the start of baking. Don't rely on how the egg yolk alone looks for doneness; the yolks should still be bright yellow (not opaque) when cooked perfectly. To check for doneness, lift an egg out of the puree a little; if the bottom of the egg feels somewhat solid, take the ramekins out of the oven and let the residual heat finish the cooking. Season to taste with additional salt and a little black pepper and serve.

POTATO GATTO
SERVES 8 TO 20 AS A MAIN COURSE,
16 TO 20 AS AN APPETIZER OR SIDE DISH

Even Italians sometimes tire of pasta, and when Neapolitans do, they turn to *gatto di patate.* This large "cake" or "gateau" (the word *gatto* is a corruption of the French word) of mashed potatoes, eggs (yolks for richness, whipped whites to lighten the texture), cheese, cured meats, and bread crumbs is exceedingly versatile. You can serve it as a main dish with vegetables—Sautéed Broccoli Rabe (page 169) and Concentrated Tomatoes (page 135) come immediately to mind—or as a side dish to chicken and meat. I, however, like it best as a casual appetizer; put the *gatto* out along with a knife and some plates and let folks help themselves. Good stuff.

MASH THE POTATOES   In a large pot of salted water, boil the potatoes whole in their jackets until just tender when pierced with a skewer. Drain and when cool enough to handle but still warm, peel and mash them, preferably with a ricer.

Heat the oven to 400°F. Coat a 10-inch springform pan or cake pan with cooking spray and coat it with a thin layer of panko. Combine the potatoes with the egg yolks, butter, Parmigiano, pecorino, ham, salami, and parsley. Taste and add salt, if needed (the cheeses and the meats will contribute salt).

WHIP THE EGG WHITES   In a stand mixer or by hand, whisk the egg whites to medium peaks. Gently fold the whites into the potato mixture. (If the mixture feels very stiff, add some warm milk, a tablespoon at a time.)

LAYER AND BAKE   Spread half of the potato mixture into the cake pan. Combine the fresh and smoked mozzarella and distribute them evenly over the potato mixture. Cover with the rest of the potato, evening the top layer with a spatula. Sprinkle the remaining panko over the top and dot with a few small pieces of butter. Bake until the

Kosher salt

3¹/4 pounds Yukon gold potatoes

Nonstick cooking spray

¹/2 cup panko, pulsed in a food
    processor

4 large egg yolks

3 tablespoons unsalted butter, at room
    temperature, cut into pieces, plus
    more for finishing

2¹/2 ounces Parmigiano-Reggiano,
    grated

1¹/2 ounces pecorino Romano, grated

2 ounces ham or prosciutto, finely diced

2 ounces salami, finely diced

1 tablespoon finely chopped fresh
    parsley

2 large egg whites

¹/4 cup warm milk, or more if needed

5 ounces fresh mozzarella, diced

3 ounces smoked mozzarella or other
    smoked cheese, diced

bread crumbs begin to brown, 35 to 40 minutes. Let the cake rest for 30 minutes before serving to fully melt the cheese.

TO SERVE   You have a choice here. Serve the *gatto* while still quite warm and you'll enjoy the melty texture of the cheese layer. Serve it later, at room temperature, and the flavors will be more pronounced and blended. Tough call, but because this makes a lot, you can actually have it both ways. Either way, you can slice it like a cake for hefty portions, or cut it into appetizer-size squares.

CHILLED CRAB SALAD WITH GINGER AND CHIVES SERVES 4

This really could not be more simple to make, yet the gingery heat combined with the crispness of the cucumbers makes it a standout.

MAKE THE CRAB SALAD   In a medium bowl, combine 1½ teaspoons lemon juice and 2 tablespoons of the olive oil. Add the cucumber and let it marinate for a few minutes. Add the ginger and combine well. Add the crabmeat and toss gently, seasoning it lightly with salt and pepper and a little more lemon juice if you like. If your ingredients were not cold to start with, chill the crab salad briefly in the refrigerator.

TO SERVE   Toss the greens with the remaining tablespoon of olive oil and season lightly with salt and pepper. Divide the greens among four plates, then mound a portion of the crab salad over the greens. Garnish with the chive batons and a tiny pinch of sea salt and serve.

$1^{1}/_{2}$ teaspoons fresh lemon juice, or more to taste

3 tablespoons extra virgin olive oil

$^{1}/_{2}$ cup peeled and finely diced cucumber

$1^{1}/_{2}$ teaspoons finely grated fresh ginger

1 pound fresh lump crabmeat, picked over for shells

Kosher salt and freshly ground black pepper

4 handfuls mixed baby greens (about 6 ounces), well washed and dried

2 tablespoons chives that have been cut into 1-inch lengths

Pinch of sea salt

GRILLED SALMON, CORN, AND AVOCADO SALAD SERVES 4

This salmon salad harks back, admittedly, to the early nineties. But I still love it and make it all the time for lunch, so here it is for you to enjoy, too. If the corn is very fresh and the kernels are small, there's no need to cook them. (If the kernels are larger and tougher, blanch the corn in boiling water for a minute.) I like salmon medium-rare to medium and serve it when the center is still slightly translucent. If you cook salmon a lot, you can judge your favorite doneness by sight and feel; a salmon cooked medium will read 135°F on an instant-read thermometer.

2 teaspoons finely chopped shallot

2 teaspoons Dijon mustard

1/4 cup balsamic vinegar

2 tablespoons red wine vinegar

1 cup olive oil, plus more for brushing the salmon

Kosher salt and freshly ground black pepper

4 center-cut salmon fillets, about 6 ounces each and 1 inch thick, with skin

1 cup fresh corn kernels

1 ripe avocado, diced

1 pint cherry or grape tomatoes, cut in half

2 heads butter lettuce, well washed and dried, torn into 1- to 2-inch pieces

Marinated Shallots (recipe follows, optional)

MAKE THE VINAIGRETTE   In a medium bowl, combine the shallot, mustard, balsamic vinegar, red wine vinegar, and the 1 cup of olive oil. Whisk or shake well to combine. Season to taste with salt and pepper.

GRILL THE SALMON   Heat the grill of your choice to medium-hot, preferably with a cooler area for indirect cooking. Lightly brush the salmon with olive oil and season well with salt and pepper. Cook the salmon until nicely browned, 3 to 4 minutes per side, before moving it to the less hot area of the grill (or lowering the flame on a gas grill) to finish to medium rare, 5 to 7 minutes. (Or let the salmon gently finish in a 250°F oven to medium rare, about 15 minutes.)

TO SERVE   Toss the corn, avocado, and tomatoes with some of the vinaigrette and divide among four serving plates. Very lightly dress the lettuce with the vinaigrette, tossing with just enough to coat the leaves. Lay the salmon on top of the avocado, corn, and tomatoes and then mound the lettuce on top of the salmon. Sprinkle with Marinated Shallots, if you like, and serve.

MARINATED SHALLOTS

MAKES ABOUT $^3/_4$ CUP

A cousin of my "Pickled" Red Onions (page 69), shallots offer just a touch more sweetness. They can be used in all kinds of salads and on sandwiches and will keep, refrigerated, for a week.

3 large shallots, thinly sliced
$^1/_2$ cup red wine vinegar
1 teaspoon kosher salt

Mix all the ingredients with ½ cup water and refrigerate, covered, for at least 8 hours and up to a week.

PRESERVED TUNA AND POTATO SALAD SERVES 4

Okay, I guess you could use really high-quality imported oil-packed tuna in this dish. But my method for poaching tuna imparts a ton of flavor and is really quite easy. The preserved tuna, which will keep for up to a week in the fridge completely submerged in oil and covered tightly, is also delicious tossed with big fat white beans, added to a pasta of olives and tomatoes, or served in a sandwich topped with lemon aïoli.

FOR THE TUNA

- 1¼ pounds fresh tuna, preferably cut into a few thick steaks
- Kosher salt and freshly ground black pepper
- 3 to 4 cups extra virgin olive oil
- 8 small fresh thyme sprigs
- 3 small fresh rosemary sprigs
- ½ lemon, sliced
- 2 shallots, sliced
- 3 garlic cloves, crushed
- ½ teaspoon crushed red pepper flakes

- 1 tablespoon finely chopped shallot
- 1 teaspoon chopped fresh chives
- 1 teaspoon red wine vinegar
- 1 teaspoon Dijon mustard
- 2 tablespoons extra virgin olive oil (or the flavored oil the tuna cooked in), plus more for drizzling
- 5 ounces green beans, trimmed
- 1 pound new potatoes, small ones left whole or cut in half, larger ones cut into quarters
- ¼ cup warm chicken broth, if needed
- Sea salt
- 8 cherry tomatoes, quartered (optional)

POACH THE TUNA   Season the tuna with salt and pepper. Combine 3 cups of the olive oil, the thyme, rosemary, lemon, shallots, garlic, and red pepper flakes in a medium saucepan and cook over medium heat until the oil reaches about 140°F. Take the pan off the heat and let the aromatics steep for 15 to 20 minutes. Meanwhile, heat the oven to 250°F. Submerge the tuna in the olive oil, adding more oil if needed to cover it completely. Put the pan in the oven and bake the tuna until well cooked, about 40 minutes. To test for doneness, break into the tuna; it should be ever so slightly pink in the center, still tender, and will register about 135°F on an instant-read thermometer. If not quite done, return it to the oven for a few more minutes. Let the tuna cool to room temperature in the oil.

MAKE THE DRESSING   In a medium bowl, combine the shallot, chives, vinegar, and mustard; then whisk in the 2 tablespoons of oil.

COOK THE VEGETABLES   Boil the green beans in well-salted water until very tender. Drain well. Boil the new potatoes in well-salted water until just tender and drain well. Toss the potatoes in the dressing, adding a little chicken broth if the mixture is very dry.

TO SERVE   Divide the beans among four serving plates, drizzle with a little olive oil, season with a pinch of sea salt, and top with the potatoes. Remove the tuna from the oil and blot it on a paper towel. Flake the tuna over the potatoes. Garnish with cherry tomatoes, if you like, and serve drizzled with a little of the tuna poaching oil.

PANINI WITH MORTADELLA, "PICKLED" RED ONIONS, AND AGED PROVOLONE SERVES 2

These are not meant to be Dagwood-style sandwiches; they are small but very flavorful. You can also slice panini into smaller pieces to serve as finger food at a gathering.

Heat a panini or sandwich grill until hot (400°F to 450°F). If you don't have a panini grill, heat a grill pan or cast-iron pan over medium-low heat. Make two sandwiches, layering the mortadella, onions, and cheese with the onions in the middle. Brush the outside of the sandwiches with olive oil and grill in the press for 9 to 10 minutes; you want to crisp and brown the bread and melt the cheese a bit, but the meat need not be excessively hot. If using a pan, weight the sandwiches down with another heavy pan set on top. Cook for 2 to 3 minutes on each side, watching them carefully and adjusting the heat as needed. Cut and serve.

Four 1/2-inch slices ciabatta or other good crusty bread

6 slices mortadella

1 tablespoon "Pickled" Red Onions, or more to taste (recipe follows)

2 to 3 slices aged provolone cheese

2 to 3 tablespoons extra virgin olive oil

"PICKLED" RED ONIONS
MAKES ABOUT 1 1/2 CUPS

These onions are great to always have on hand. They will last at least a week in the fridge, and they add a tangy (and not overly oniony) note to salads and sandwiches. If, like me, you get hooked, know that the recipe is easily doubled.

2 medium red onions, thinly sliced

1 cup red wine vinegar

3 teaspoons kosher salt

Combine all the ingredients with 1 cup of water and refrigerate, covered, for at least 8 hours. Serve to accompany various salads and sandwiches.

CRISPY SWEETBREADS SALAD SERVES 4 AS A MAIN COURSE, 6 AS AN APPETIZER

Sweetbreads are often not so easy to find, but if you love them like I do, you know how to get your hands on some, whether by sweet-talking your butcher or by mail order. This recipe is a little fussy, what with the blanching and sautéing of various vegetables, but if you've gone to the trouble of seeking out sweetbreads, why not present them at their best? Here, small pieces of sweetbreads are cooked and then coated in a rich but slightly tangy sauce. The result is crispy yet slightly sticky—imagine only the best aspects of a good General Tso's chicken. I like to serve this as an appetizer salad, preferably after a lighter raw fish starter.

FOR THE SWEETBREADS

2 pounds sweetbreads, trimmed, outer membrane removed, and soaked in cold water in the refrigerator for 2 hours

1/2 onion, sliced

1 carrot, chopped

1 tablespoon black peppercorns

2 bay leaves

1 cup white wine

2 tablespoons kosher salt

FOR THE SALAD

1/4 cup fava beans

1/4 cup thinly sliced asparagus

1/4 cup peas, preferably fresh

5 tablespoons extra virgin olive oil

1/2 small carrot, finely diced (about 1/4 cup)

4 chanterelle mushrooms, cleaned and cut into small pieces (about 1/4 cup)

1 small fresh thyme sprig

POACH THE SWEETBREADS   Remove the sweetbreads from the cold water, rinse, and pat dry. In a large saucepan, bring 6 cups of water, the onion, carrot, peppercorns, bay leaves, wine, and salt to a boil. Reduce to a gentle simmer and let the ingredients steep for 25 minutes. Add the sweetbreads and simmer until rare, 12 to 15 minutes. (The inside of the sweetbreads will be pinkish and milky.) Remove the sweetbreads from the poaching liquid and let cool slightly. When you are able to handle them, remove any tough membranes or blood vessels as you tear the sweetbreads into their naturally occurring smaller lobes, each about the size of a thumbnail. (You can poach and tear the sweetbreads a few hours before assembling the final dish; keep them covered and refrigerated.)

PREPARE THE VEGETABLES   Bring a small saucepan of water to a boil and set a bowl of ice water nearby. Blanch the fava beans for a minute and then immediately plunge them into the ice water. Scoop them out with a slotted spoon and peel their tough skins by pinching them between your thumb and finger. Blanch and shock the asparagus and the peas in the same manner. Heat a tablespoon of the olive oil over medium-high heat and sauté the carrot and mushrooms until just lightly golden. Set aside.

I was in a springtime mood when I wrote this, but feel free to switch the accompaniments to butternut squash or pumpkin, prunes or raisins, or all of them.

FRY THE SWEETBREADS   Heat 3 tablespoons of the olive oil in a large sauté pan over medium-high heat. Add the sweetbreads and pan-fry them until crispy. Remove them from the pan and drain off the oil. Put a little fresh olive oil in the pan and add all of the vegetables and the thyme. Cook over medium heat for a couple of minutes to meld their flavors. Return the sweetbreads to the pan along with the chicken reduction and the vinegar. Cook until the liquid reduces, coating the sweetbreads and making them glisten. You want most of the liquid in the pan gone.

TO SERVE   Divide the vegetables and sweetbreads among six plates. Top with the baby greens and the chives. Using a vegetable peeler, finish each plate with a few shavings of Parmigiano. Serve immediately.

$^1/_4$ cup Chicken Reduction (page 242) or good-quality purchased chicken base, reconstituted as the package directs until a little thicker than chicken broth

1 tablespoon red wine vinegar

6 handfuls mixed baby greens (about 8 ounces), well washed and dried

3 teaspoons chopped fresh chives

1 ounce Parmigiano-Reggiano

SMOKED HAM, ROASTED RADICCHIO, AND CHEESE PANINI, page 74

SMOKED HAM, ROASTED RADICCHIO, AND CHEESE PANINI SERVES 2

Why settle for plain old ham and cheese when you can easily make this panini? You will have some roasted radicchio left over, which is fine since it makes a nice addition to a green salad and will keep a few days in the refrigerator.

1 head radicchio, cut through the core into 8 wedges

1/4 cup extra virgin olive oil

Kosher salt and freshly ground black pepper

Four 1/2-inch slices ciabatta or other good crusty bread

6 thin slices smoked ham

2 to 3 ounces assertive cheese, such as Gorgonzola or Camembert, crumbled or thinly sliced

ROAST THE RADICCHIO Heat the oven to 350°F. Lay the wedges of radicchio on a small sheet pan and drizzle with about 2 tablespoons of the olive oil. Season with salt and pepper and cover the pan with aluminum foil. (Covering the pan allows the radicchio to steam and roast at the same time.) Cook until very tender and lightly browned, about 30 minutes. (The radicchio can be roasted a day ahead.)

GRILL THE PANINI Heat a panini or sandwich grill until hot (400°F to 450°F). If you don't have a panini grill, heat a grill pan or cast-iron pan over medium-low heat. Pat the radicchio dry, if need be, and cut away any tough core. Make two sandwiches, layering the ham, cheese, and radicchio. (You may not use all of the radicchio.)

Brush the outsides of the sandwiches with olive oil and grill in the press for 9 to 10 minutes; you want to crisp and brown the bread and melt the cheese a bit, but the meat need not be excessively hot. If using a pan, weight the sandwiches down with another heavy pan set on top. Cook for 2 to 3 minutes on each side, watching them carefully and adjusting the heat as needed. Cut and serve.

GRILLED SAUSAGE SANDWICHES WITH SPINACH AND PROVOLONE SERVES 6 TO 8

Sausage and peppers are great, but you pretty much can't beat the ones off the carts, whether in Manhattan or Boston. So here's a sandwich that similarly satisfies, but is just a tad more refined. I'll double this and make it when I have some friends over to watch a football game; we call it "fat bastard" food.

GRILL THE SAUSAGE   Heat the grill of your choice until medium hot. Grill the sausages, turning them occasionally, until browned and crisped on the outside and just fully cooked within, about 10 minutes. Transfer to a cutting board.

WILT THE SPINACH   Heat a large sauté pan over medium heat. Add the olive oil and garlic and cook slowly until the garlic is floating and lightly sizzling. Add the spinach, season lightly with salt, and cook, gently tossing the spinach, until fully wilted. Remove from heat.

TO SERVE   Slice the sausages as you like to eat them on a sandwich (lengthwise or into rounds; it's up to you) and add to the spinach. Cook over medium heat, tossing until the flavors have mingled and all is hot, about 2 minutes. Take the pan off the heat and sprinkle on the provolone. Divide the mixture among the rolls and serve.

2 pounds sweet or spicy Italian sausage or a mix of both

1 tablespoon extra virgin olive oil

2 garlic cloves, very thinly sliced

10 ounces fresh spinach or broccoli rabe, well washed and dried, thick stems removed, coarsely chopped

Kosher salt

4 ounces provolone, grated or shredded

8 fist-size rolls, preferably ciabatta, split

Pasta, Risotto, and Gnocchi

The starches. Italians have the best way with starches, transforming flour and eggs into exquisite pastas, mashed potatoes into supple gnocchi, and plain old rice into regal risotto. Here I present recipes that run the gamut, from the most basic of all pastas—spaghetti with garlic and olive oil (page 78), made the *right* way—to handmade, meat-filled plin (page 100), an exquisite dish best saved for special occasions.

I really hope that my fresh pasta recipes inspire you to make your own pasta dough. Few foods are as rewarding to serve to friends and family as homemade pasta. It is unexpected and utterly appreciated.

The key to making pasta by hand is losing the anxiety surrounding it. For example, people who don't make fresh pasta often (or at all) tend to handle the dough as if it were the most fragile thing in the world. Guess what? It's not. It's true that you don't want to add so much flour that it becomes tough, but if a sheet sticks to the pasta machine during rolling, do not hesitate to flour it well before continuing. Also, many fresh pasta recipes instruct you to roll pasta "to its thinnest setting." But because pasta machines vary, you should not feel obliged to do that; you'll know whether the pasta you made that day—and all pasta doughs will vary depending on your flour, your eggs, the weather—will make it through the next thinnest setting. For most fresh pastas, you should stop rolling when you can easily see the outline of your hand through the dough. Finally, make the filling or sauce on a different day from the pasta; the enterprise will feel much less arduous that way. And don't forget to put on the music while you're in the kitchen. Some Willie Nelson on the stereo will calm even the most nervous of pasta makers.

SPAGHETTI WITH GARLIC AND OLIVE OIL SERVES 2

No pasta could be easier than spaghetti and olive oil, right? Yet I can't believe how badly this sublime and simple pasta gets made, with not enough oil, undercooked garlic, and the addition of cheese, which I think is sinful. Here's my spaghetti *agli' olio.*

Kosher salt

1/4 cup extra virgin olive oil

1/2 pound dried spaghetti

3 garlic cloves, very thinly sliced

Pinch of crushed red pepper flakes

2 tablespoons chopped fresh parsley, or more to taste (optional)

Bring a large pot of well-salted water to a boil. Heat the olive oil in a sauté pan over medium heat. Start boiling the spaghetti. While it cooks, sauté the garlic over just enough heat that it sizzles gently. Add the red pepper flakes. When the edges of the garlic just start to brown, add 1 cup of the pasta water and a pinch of salt. Keep cooking, shaking the pan to create an emulsion, until the oil and water mixture no longer has that harsh raw-garlic flavor.

When the pasta is al dente, drain it and add it to the pan, along with the chopped parsley, if using, tossing to coat. Serve immediately.

SPAGHETTI WITH CLAMS SERVES 2 TO 3

This dish has only a passing resemblance to your more typical "linguine with clam sauce." For starters, there's no wine. I hate wine in clam sauce. This may stem from my days in a restaurant kitchen where we had a box of cheap wine near the stove. When we cooked clams, we'd put the pan under the wine spout and, using tongs to flick the tap, were encouraged to let the wine flow into the pan. The alcohol never got cooked off, and the dish always tasted more of wine than of clams. Here, I combine the pasta and clams before either is fully cooked. As the clams open, they release their juices, which the spaghetti soaks up to become full of that deliciously briny flavor. The final result may look a little drier than you're used to, but the hope is that you will experience a more pure clam flavor.

WASH THE CLAMS   Put the clams in a large bowl of water and agitate the water with your hands. Let any grit settle to the bottom and then lift the clams out of the bowl.

COOK THE PASTA   Bring a large pot of salted water to a boil. Add the pasta and cook until only about three-quarters done; you should still see some white in the center of the spaghetti when you bite it. Reserve about 1 cup of the pasta water, then drain the pasta.

MAKE THE "SAUCE"   While the spaghetti cooks, heat the ¼ cup of olive oil in a large, high-sided sauté pan over medium heat. When hot, add the garlic and take the pan off the heat. Add the red pepper flakes and swirl the garlic around in the pan to prevent it from overcooking. Add ¾ cup of the pasta water to the pan and bring to a boil over medium-high heat for a minute to create an emulsion. Add the pasta and the clams, cover, and cook until the clams open up and the pasta is al dente, adding more water only if needed, about 5 minutes.

TO SERVE   Add the parsley to the pan and toss. Drizzle with the tablespoon of olive oil, season with additional salt if needed, and serve immediately.

1 3/4 pounds Manila or littleneck clams (about 28)

Kosher salt

1/2 pound dried spaghetti

1/4 cup plus 1 tablespoon olive oil

3 garlic cloves, very thinly sliced

Large pinch of crushed red pepper flakes

1/3 cup chopped fresh parsley

BRAISED SNAILS WITH MUSHROOMS AND MACCHERONI SERVES 4

You can buy canned snails (*lumache* in Italian) at most supermarkets; if you have a choice, buy the smaller size, which are more tender when cooked. As for the pasta, I like to use an imported, squared spaghetti-like pasta about six inches long. (It's similar to *maccheroni alla chitarra,* which is made by pressing the pasta dough through guitarlike strings.) A good-quality thick spaghetti or a thin penne would also work well here.

One 7.75-ounce can snails, drained and rinsed

1/2 cup dry white wine

2 cups Chicken Broth (page 241)

2 medium shallots, 1 finely chopped and 1 thinly sliced

1 teaspoon finely chopped fresh rosemary

3 tablespoons extra virgin olive oil

5 ounces mushrooms, preferably wild (I like a mix of shiitake and porcini), sliced or cut into naturally occurring pieces

1/8 to 1/4 teaspoon crushed red pepper flakes

Kosher salt

1/2 pound dried thick spaghetti, broken in half

1 plum tomato, peeled, seeded, and finely diced

1 tablespoon finely grated Parmigiano-Reggiano

Chives, cut into 1-inch lengths, for garnish (about 1 tablespoon)

BRAISE THE SNAILS   In a medium saucepan, combine the snails, wine, chicken broth, chopped shallot, and rosemary. Bring the ingredients to a boil, reduce to a simmer, cover, and cook until the snails are very tender, about 45 minutes. Drain the snails, reserving them with their cooking liquid. (The snails can be cooked a day ahead, refrigerated, then reheated very gently.)

SAUTÉ THE MUSHROOMS   Heat a large sauté pan over medium-high heat. Add about 1 tablespoon of the olive oil and cook the sliced shallot until soft, about 5 minutes. Add the mushrooms and another tablespoon of olive oil and cook until the mushrooms are lightly browned, about 5 minutes. Add the red pepper flakes, the snails, and 1 cup of the snail braising liquid. Stir to mix. Remove the snails from the heat but keep them warm.

COOK THE PASTA   Bring a large pot of well-salted water to a boil. Cook the pasta until al dente. Reserve about 1/2 cup of the pasta water, then drain the pasta. Add the pasta and the tomato to the snails and mushrooms, and cook over medium heat, stirring, to let the flavors combine. Add a little more liquid (either more snail braising liquid or the pasta water) if the mixture looks dry.

TO SERVE   Stir in the remaining tablespoon of oil. Divide the pasta among four warm bowls and sprinkle with cheese and chives.

PENNE WITH ROASTED PUMPKIN, ESCAROLE, AND MUSHROOMS SERVES 4 TO 6

At first the escarole will seem like too much, but it cooks down to the perfect amount. This is a lovely, full-flavored vegetarian dish for fall.

ROAST THE PUMPKIN   Heat the oven to 400°F. Trim, peel, and seed the pumpkin. Cut it into small (⅓-inch) cubes to yield about 2 cups. On a small sheet pan, toss the pumpkin with about 2 tablespoons of the olive oil and a pinch of the red pepper flakes. Season with salt and pepper and roast until browned and tender but still holds its shape, about 10 minutes.

COOK THE ESCAROLE AND MUSHROOMS   In a large sauté pan, heat 1½ to 2 tablespoons of the olive oil over medium-high heat. When the oil begins to shimmer, add the garlic and red pepper flakes. Take the pan off the heat, stirring or swirling the garlic to prevent scorching, until the garlic is very fragrant and just starts to take on some color. Return the pan to the heat, add the mushrooms, season with ample salt and pepper, and cook, stirring, until the mushrooms release most of their liquid, about 4 minutes. Add the escarole and cook, stirring until wilted. Add the roasted squash and keep warm.

COOK THE PASTA   Meanwhile, bring a large pot of well-salted water to a boil and cook the pasta until just al dente. Reserve about 1 cup of the pasta water, then drain the pasta. Add the pasta and about ¼ cup of the reserved water to the pan with the escarole and heat over medium-high heat while tossing everything together well. Taste and season again with salt and pepper. If the sauce looks too dry, add a bit more of the cooking liquid.

TO SERVE   Divide the pasta among four or six warm bowls and sprinkle each with some parsley and cheese.

1 small pumpkin or butternut squash

3 to 4 tablespoons extra virgin olive oil

¼ teaspoon crushed red pepper flakes, plus more to taste

Kosher salt and freshly ground black pepper

5 garlic cloves, very thinly sliced

8 ounces domestic or wild mushrooms (a mix is nice), wiped clean, stemmed, and sliced or broken into bite-size pieces

1 medium head escarole (about 1 pound), any wilted outer leaves discarded, well washed and dried, and chopped into 1- or 2-inch pieces

¾ pound dried penne

Chopped fresh parsley

¼ cup grated Parmigiano-Reggiano

CAVATELLI WITH WILTED GREENS, CRISPY PANCETTA, AND CHICKPEAS SERVES 4 TO 6

Salty pancetta and bitter greens get tamed by the addition of earthy chickpeas in this hearty pasta. I like to use dandelion greens in this dish.

Kosher salt

2 tablespoons extra virgin olive oil

4 ounces pancetta, diced

2 medium shallots, thinly sliced

One 15-ounce can chickpeas (about 1²/3 cups)

1 small bunch mustard greens or other bitter greens, trimmed of tough stems, well washed, and coarsely chopped (about 2 cups)

1 pound fresh or frozen cavatelli

1/4 cup grated Parmigiano-Reggiano, or more to taste

Bring a large pot of well-salted water to a boil.

CRISP THE PANCETTA   Heat 1 tablespoon of the olive oil in a large sauté pan over medium-high heat. Add the pancetta and cook, stirring occasionally, until crisp. Remove the pancetta with a slotted spoon (but do not clean the pan) and reserve.

COOK THE VEGETABLES   Add the other tablespoon of oil to the pan and heat it over medium heat. Add the shallots and cook, stirring occasionally, until tender. Add the chickpeas and the greens, season lightly with salt, and cook until the greens have wilted, about 3 minutes.

COOK THE PASTA   Meanwhile, cook the cavatelli in the boiling water until just shy of al dente. Reserve about 1 cup of the cooking water, then drain the pasta. Add the pasta, pancetta, and ½ cup of the pasta water to the chickpeas and greens. Cook, adding more of the pasta water if the mixture looks dry, until the pasta is al dente.

TO SERVE   Add the Parmigiano and toss again. Serve immediately with additional cheese, if you like.

TAGLIATELLE WITH PEAS AND PROSCIUTTO SERVES 4

The striking look of this pasta belies how easy it is to make and how accessible its ingredients are. If you're feeling fancy, however, finish the pasta with some truffle butter, about a teaspoon per serving. Serve this to celebrate the start of spring.

Bring a large pot of well-salted water to a boil.

MAKE A PEA PUREE   In a small saucepan, heat 1 tablespoon of olive oil over medium heat. Add the shallot, season with a generous pinch of salt, and cook until tender, about 5 minutes. Add half the peas and the chicken broth. Increase the heat to medium-high and cook the peas until tender, 2 to 3 minutes. Add the parsley and tarragon. Transfer the mixture to a blender or food processor (or use a hand blender right in the pot) and puree it. (Rewarm it before serving and thin it with a little broth if necessary.)

CRISP THE PROSCIUTTO   Heat about a teaspoon of olive oil in a medium sauté pan. Add the prosciutto and cook, stirring occasionally, until the prosciutto is quite crispy, 4 to 5 minutes.

COOK THE PASTA   If using fresh pasta, add it and the other half of the peas to the boiling water at the same time and cook until the pasta is al dente. If using dried, start the pasta first and add the peas for the last 2 minutes of cooking. Reserve a cup or so of the pasta water, then drain the pasta and peas. Return the pasta and peas to the pot they were cooked in, add the pea puree, and toss to coat, adding a little of the reserved pasta water if it looks dry.

TO SERVE   Divide the pasta among warm bowls and top with the prosciutto. Drizzle a teaspoon of olive oil over each bowl and serve immediately topped with Parmigiano-Reggiano if you like.

Kosher salt

Extra virgin olive oil

1 shallot, thinly sliced lengthwise

1 cup fresh or frozen peas

1 1/2 cups Chicken Broth (page 241)

1 teaspoon chopped fresh parsley

2 teaspoons chopped fresh tarragon

4 thin slices prosciutto, chopped

3/4 pound fresh or dried tagliatelle

1/4 cup grated Parmigiano-Reggiano (optional)

FETTUCCINE WITH SPECK, POTATOES, AND BROCCOLI RABE SERVES 4

Because my cooking has of late been focused on northern Italy, potatoes seem to be popping up everywhere, including in a few of my favorite pastas. Speck, a delicious cured ham, also hails from northern Italy, specifically Alto Adige, where it's famously produced. You can find speck at a good Italian market or a specialty food store, though it will likely come from Austria and not Italy. Pancetta or prosciutto can substitute for the speck, if you can't find it.

1 tablespoon plus 1 teaspoon extra virgin olive oil

1 tablespoon unsalted butter

2 shallots, finely chopped

Kosher salt

$1^2/_3$ cups diced potatoes (4 medium fingerlings or 2 to 3 Yukon golds)

Leaves from 4 small fresh thyme sprigs

Pinch of crushed red pepper flakes

$1^1/_2$ to 2 cups Chicken Broth (page 241), plus more if needed

2 slices speck, pancetta, or prosciutto, julienned

$3/_4$ pound fresh or dried fettuccine

1 small bunch broccoli rabe, blanched

3 tablespoons grated Parmigiano-Reggiano

COOK THE POTATOES In a large sauté pan, heat the tablespoon of olive oil and the butter over medium heat. Add the shallots and a pinch of salt, and cook until tender but not colored, about 5 minutes. Add the potatoes, thyme, red pepper flakes, and enough broth to cover the potatoes. Bring to a gentle boil, reduce to a simmer, and cook until the potatoes are just shy of tender, about 7 minutes. Take the pan off the heat and reserve.

CRISP THE SPECK Meanwhile, heat the teaspoon of olive oil in a small sauté pan and cook the speck over medium-low heat until lightly browned.

COOK THE PASTA Bring a large pot of well-salted water to a boil. Cook the pasta until just shy of tender. While the pasta is cooking, add the broccoli rabe to the potatoes and reheat if necessary. Drain the pasta and toss it with the vegetables. Continue to cook over medium-high heat until the potatoes are tender and the pasta is al dente, about 5 minutes, allowing the stock to cook down.

TO SERVE Take the pan off the heat, toss in the speck and the cheese, and serve.

PAPPARDELLE WITH DUCK RAGU AND BLACK OLIVES SERVES 6

This recipe looks long and involved, but most of the ingredients are tossed into a single pan and then left in the oven to cook into a rich ragu that can be made a couple of days before you plan to serve the pasta. The payoff is much greater—more deeply flavored and full bodied—if you use a reduced chicken stock. Try my Chicken Reduction or a good-quality purchased chicken base, such as More Than Gourmet's Glace de Poulet Gold (Classic Roasted Chicken Stock), reconstituted as the package directs.

BRAISE THE DUCK   Heat the oven to 350°F. Heat a large ovenproof sauté pan or small roasting pan over medium-high heat. Season the duck legs with salt and pepper and put them in the pan, skin side down. Cook, in batches if necessary, until the duck is golden brown and all of the fat has rendered, about 12 minutes. (You may need to carefully pour the fat from the pan as the legs sear; save the duck fat to strain and use in other cooking, if you like.)

Set the legs aside and reserve 1 tablespoon of the duck fat for this recipe. Return the pan to the heat and add the 1 tablespoon of fat, the onion, celery, carrot, and garlic. Reduce the heat to medium and cook, stirring, until the vegetables are lightly browned, about 3 minutes. Add the wine and vinegar and cook, stirring to scrape up the juices stuck to the bottom of the pan, until the liquid has reduced by about one-third, about 4 minutes. Add the chicken reduction, tomatoes, thyme, rosemary, and sage. Cook, stirring occasionally, for 2 minutes.

Return the duck legs to the pan and bring to a gentle boil. Cover with a lid or with aluminum foil and braise in the oven until the meat easily pulls off the bones, about 1 hour. Remove the legs from the pan and set aside until cool enough to handle. Strain the sauce through a fine strainer and reserve; if using right away, spoon off the

4 whole, skin-on duck legs (about 3^1/4 pounds), trimmed of excess fat and skin

Kosher salt and freshly ground black pepper

^{1}/2 small onion, chopped

^{1}/2 celery stalk, chopped

^{1}/2 carrot, chopped

1 garlic clove, chopped

^{1}/3 cup red wine

^{1}/3 cup red wine vinegar

1^1/2 cups Chicken Reduction (page 242) or good-quality purchased chicken base, reconstituted as the package directs until a little thicker than chicken broth

2 canned plum tomatoes, seeded and chopped

2 small fresh thyme sprigs

1 small fresh rosemary sprig

1 small fresh sage sprig

^{1}/2 cup oil-cured black olives

1 pound pappardelle, preferably fresh

2 tablespoons chopped fresh parsley, or more to taste

2 tablespoons grated Parmigiano-Reggiano, or more to taste

fat visible on top. (If not using immediately, you can more easily remove the fat, which will solidify, after the sauce has been chilled overnight in the refrigerator.) Remove the meat from the legs, shredding it with your fingers into bite-size pieces, and reserve. (The duck can be braised a day or two ahead; moisten the meat with a little of the sauce and refrigerate the sauce and meat separately.)

TO FINISH   Bring a large pot of well-salted water to a boil. Meanwhile, reheat the sauce in a medium saucepan over medium-high heat. Let it bubble away for a few minutes to reduce in volume and intensify in flavor. Add the reserved duck meat and the olives to the sauce, reduce the heat to medium-low, and cook until the duck is thoroughly heated.

Cook the pappardelle until al dente and drain. Return the pasta to the pot it cooked in. With a slotted spoon, add all of the duck meat and olives to the pasta. Then add as much of the sauce as needed to make a moist but not overly wet ragu. Add the parsley and the cheese and toss to combine.

TO SERVE   Divide the pasta among six warm bowls, spoon a little more sauce over the top, sprinkle with additional parsley and cheese if you like, and serve immediately.

FRESH PASTA DOUGH
MAKES ABOUT $1^1/2$ POUNDS OF DOUGH

The amount of flour you use will vary every time you make fresh pasta because of variables in different flours, the size of your eggs, and even the weather. We chefs tend to warn so much about overdoing it with the flour that people often go too far the other way, resulting in frustratingly sticky dough that is hard, if not impossible, to roll. The key is not to add too much flour at once. Instead, add it gradually as needed. Keep your work surfaces well floured, too.

3 to 3¹/₂ cups "00" or all-purpose flour, plus more
     for rolling and shaping
1 teaspoon kosher salt
4 large eggs
2 large egg yolks
1 teaspoon olive oil

MIX THE DOUGH   On a clean counter, whisk together 3 cups of the flour and the salt. Make a deep and wide well in the center of the flour. (You may not need all of the flour, but the extra helps keep the eggs contained within the well; it's a drag if the eggs escape and run all over.)

Combine the eggs, yolks, and olive oil in the center of the well and whisk to combine. Without breaking the wall, gradually mix in the flour with a fork a little at a time until the eggs are no longer runny. Stay mainly in the center of the well as you mix. Continue to bring in more and more flour until the dough becomes too stiff to work with a fork. At this point, use your hands to bring in just enough of the remaining flour to make a cohesive mass. When the dough no longer easily absorbs more flour, set the dough aside, scrape the work surface clean of excess flour and dried bits of dough, and wash and dry your hands.

KNEAD THE DOUGH   Lightly reflour the clean work surface and knead the dough until it's smooth and homogenous, about 5 minutes. You'll know you have added the right amount of flour and kneaded long enough when the dough no longer sticks to a clean finger and feels resilient. Wrap the dough well in plastic and let it rest in the refrigerator for at least an hour before rolling it.

ROLL THE DOUGH   Take the dough out of the fridge and let it warm up a bit. Get your pasta machine ready with the roller set to the widest setting. Flour your work surface. Cut the pasta dough into 4 pieces. Very lightly flour one piece (cover the rest with plastic wrap) and run it through the pasta machine on the widest setting two times. Fold it in half and run it through again. Fold it in half again and run it through again. Set the machine to the next level of thickness and run the piece of dough through. Lightly flour the dough if it seems sticky during the rolling. (If it tears, flour it and repeat on a wider setting.) Continue rolling the dough on each successively narrower setting until it's about $\frac{1}{32}$ inch thick and you can see the shape of your hand through the sheet (the actual setting will vary by machine). Be sure you have a lot of work space, as the pasta sheets will get quite long. You can stack the sheets of dough if you flour them well, or cover each in plastic wrap.

Repeat this entire process with the remaining three pieces of dough. Use the rolled pasta sheets as directed in the specific recipe.

NOTE   If a recipe calls for a half batch of pasta dough or less, you can either cut the recipe in half or—the better option in my opinion—make the whole batch and cut the remaining sheets of pasta into fettuccine, pappardelle, or tagliatelle. (Use the cutter that came with your pasta machine or a large, sharp knife.) Wrap the cut pasta loosely around your hand to make a nest and freeze the nests on a parchment-lined baking sheet. When they are rock solid, you can transfer them to a zip-top bag for easier storage in the freezer.

RICOTTA RAVIOLINI WITH ANCHOVY BUTTER AND ZUCCHINI SERVES 4

Nothing beats homemade pasta, but you can also try this anchovy butter on good-quality purchased ravioli. If you can get zucchini blossoms—they're often at farmers' markets—slice a few thinly and add them toward the end of cooking for a beautiful burst of color. Some people can't get enough of anchovies while for others, a little goes a long way; if you fall into the latter group, leave some of the actual anchovies behind in the pan when you pour the anchovy butter over the pasta. If you love anchovies, scrape the pan to make sure you get every last bit!

MAKE THE ANCHOVY BUTTER In a medium sauté pan, heat 1 tablespoon of the olive oil over medium heat. Add the anchovies and cook, smashing them with the back of a spoon and swirling them in the pan, until they practically melt. Add 3 tablespoons of butter. Cook, stirring, until the butter melts; keep the anchovy butter warm.

COOK THE VEGETABLES In a large, high-sided sauté pan, heat the remaining tablespoon of olive oil over medium heat. Add the shallots and red pepper flakes and cook until the shallots are tender and lightly browned, about 7 minutes. Add the zucchini, a little salt, and cook for about 1 minute. Increase the heat to medium-high, add ¾ cup water, and cook until just crisp-tender, about 2 minutes.

COOK THE PASTA Bring a large pot of well-salted water to a boil. Cook the raviolini at a gentle boil until just tender. Reserve some of the pasta water and gently drain the raviolini. Add the pasta to the pan with the zucchini along with the remaining tablespoon of butter, the parsley, and the zucchini blossoms, if using. Toss gently, adding a little of the pasta water if the dish looks very dry, and keep warm over low heat.

TO SERVE Reheat the anchovy butter over medium-high heat. Drizzle it over the pasta and serve immediately.

2 tablespoons extra virgin olive oil

4 whole anchovies (or 8 fillets), backbone removed if whole, rinsed well and patted dry

4 tablespoons (1/2 stick) unsalted butter at room temperature

2 medium shallots, thinly sliced

Pinch of crushed red pepper flakes

2 baby zucchini, julienned (if you use larger, don't use the seedy interior), to yield about 1 scant cup

Kosher salt

Ricotta Raviolini (recipe follows) or 1 pound good-quality purchased cheese ravioli, preferably about 1 inch wide

2 teaspoons chopped fresh parsley

4 zucchini blossoms (optional), thinly sliced

RICOTTA RAVIOLINI

MAKES ABOUT 100 RAVIOLINI

These tiny ravioli are delicious with all kinds of toppings, including the Cherry Tomato Sauce on page 19 and the Fresh Tomato Sauce on page 122.

8 ounces fresh ricotta
2 egg yolks
1 ounce Parmigiano-Reggiano, finely grated
Kosher salt and freshly ground white pepper
$^1/_2$ batch ($^3/_4$ pound) Fresh Pasta Dough (page 88)

MAKE THE FILLING Combine the ricotta, egg yolks, Parmigiano-Reggiano, and salt and pepper to taste, and mix well.

FILL AND FREEZE Roll the dough into very thin sheets following the directions that came with your pasta machine or those on page 90. (You want the sheets thin enough so that you can see the shape of your hand through the dough.)

If you have a ravioli mold with tiny squares, use it following the manufacturer's directions. If you don't have a mold, very lightly brush the sheet of pasta with water. Place dots of filling (about a half teaspoon each) at 1-inch intervals just below *and* just above the middle of the sheet. (You can use a pastry bag to do this if that's easier; just be sure the opening is big enough to accommodate the filling.) Carefully lift the bottom edge of the sheet and bring it to meet the middle, letting it fall loosely over the bottom row of filling. Then bring the top edge of the dough down over the top row of filling to meet the middle. Using the pinky side of each hand, gently pat the area close to each lump of filling to coax out any trapped air. Flour a pastry cutter and cut tiny squares around each mound of filling.

Line a sided baking sheet with parchment paper and flour the paper. As you work, transfer the filled pasta to the baking sheet in a single layer. (Don't stack them or they will stick together.) Freeze the raviolini on the baking sheet until they feel rock solid, then transfer them to freezer bags or other airtight containers for longer storage. (They'll keep, frozen, for up to 2 weeks.) If you prefer to cook the raviolini right away, freeze them for as long as you can so they don't swell too much when boiled.

BURRATA CANNELLONI   SERVES 6; MAKES 18 TO 20 CANNELLONI

This cannelloni is both special-occasion fare and soothing comfort food. Buttery, creamy burrata cheese is what makes my cannelloni outstanding, but it's not easy to find. (See Sources.) Though you could substitute the same amount of ricotta cheese for the burrata, the payoff for making the cannelloni won't be as big.

$^1/_2$ recipe Fresh Pasta Dough (page 88)

1 pound burrata cheese

$^1/_4$ cup fresh ricotta

3 egg yolks

$^1/_4$ cup fine, dry bread crumbs, preferably panko

2 tablespoons chopped fresh parsley

$^1/_2$ teaspoon finely chopped fresh mint

Kosher salt and freshly ground black pepper

2 tablespoons extra virgin olive oil, plus more for drizzling over the pasta

1 pint cherry tomatoes, cut in half

$^1/_2$ teaspoon chopped fresh oregano

$^2/_3$ cup Fresh Tomato Sauce (page 122) or other good-quality, lightly seasoned tomato sauce

1 tablespoon unsalted butter, cut into tiny pieces

2 tablespoons finely grated Parmigiano-Reggiano

PARCOOK THE PASTA   Roll the dough into very thin sheets following the directions that came with your pasta machine or those on page 90. (You want the sheets thin enough so that you can see the shape of your hand through the dough.) Bring a large pot of well-salted water to a boil; have a bowl filled with ice water near the stove. Also have out some clean towels. Cut the sheets into more manageable lengths of about 12 inches and boil them, in batches, until just barely al dente, about 1 minute. (Reserve a cup of the pasta water to thin the sauce, if needed.) Carefully transfer the sheets to the ice water to stop their cooking. Drain well by laying the pasta sheets on the towels.

MAKE THE FILLING   Combine the burrata cheese with the ricotta, egg yolks, bread crumbs, parsley, and mint. Season to taste with salt and pepper.

COOK THE SAUCE   Heat the 2 tablespoons of olive oil in a large sauté pan over medium to medium-high heat. Add the tomatoes, the oregano, some salt, and a touch of pepper. Cook the tomatoes until most of their juices have reduced so that there is little liquid left in the pan, about 10 minutes. Add the tomato sauce and bring to a boil. Reduce the heat and keep the tomatoes warm.

STUFF THE PASTA   You can make the cannelloni one at a time or a few at a time, whichever is easier for you.

To make them one at a time, cut the dry sheets of pasta into 20 rectangles measuring about 4 by 5 inches; you may not need all of the pasta. Lay a ½-inch-thick line of filling along the shorter side, about ¾ inch from the edge. (You can use a pastry bag to do this if that's easier.) Gently roll the pasta around the filling until you have a compact tube.

To make more than one at a time, trim a sheet of pasta so that its short side is about 5 inches. Lay the filling along the long side of the sheet and roll the pasta around the filling. Cut this long tube into individual cannelloni.

Transfer the cannelloni to a baking dish, fitting them in snugly, seam side down.

BAKE THE PASTA   Heat the oven to 325°F. Drizzle the cannelloni with a little olive oil and dot them all over with the butter. Sprinkle the grated cheese, about ½ teaspoon per portion, over them evenly. Bake until very lightly browned on top and heated through, 10 to 15 minutes. Meanwhile, reheat the tomato sauce over medium heat, adding a little of the reserved pasta cooking water if very thick.

TO SERVE   Just before taking the cannelloni out of the oven, spoon about ½ cup sauce on each serving dish and place the cannelloni, 3 per person, on top of the cheese.

BURRATA CANNELLONI, page 94

EGGPLANT AND TALEGGIO MEZZALUNA

SERVES 6; MAKES ABOUT 70 MEZZALUNA

These "half-moon" filled pastas show off the complementary flavors of eggplant and creamy, full-flavored Taleggio cheese. Serve them with the Cherry Tomato Sauce, made without the basil.

FOR THE FILLING

1 medium eggplant, cut into $1/2$-inch dice

1 teaspoon kosher salt, or more to taste

2 to 3 tablespoons olive oil

4 shallots, thinly sliced

3 fresh thyme sprigs

5 plum tomatoes, seeded and diced

1 cup Chicken Broth (page 241)

4 ounces Taleggio cheese, frozen briefly to make shredding easier

1 tablespoon chopped fresh parsley

FOR THE PASTA

Fresh Pasta Dough (page 88)

All-purpose flour for rolling the dough

Cherry Tomato Sauce (page 19), made without the basil

2 tablespoons unsalted butter

2 to 3 tablespoons grated Parmigiano-Reggiano, plus shavings for garnish

2 to 3 teaspoons snipped fresh chives

SALT THE EGGPLANT   Put the eggplant in a colander and toss with the teaspoon of salt. Put the colander in a clean sink, weight the eggplant, and allow the salt to draw out the excess moisture for 30 minutes. Pat the eggplant dry.

MAKE THE FILLING   In a deep-sided skillet or sauté pan, heat about 2 tablespoons of the olive oil over medium-high heat. Add the shallots and sauté until lightly browned on the edges. Add the eggplant to the pan along with the thyme and additional olive oil if needed. Lower the heat to medium and sweat the eggplant, stirring occasionally, for about 6 minutes. Add the tomatoes and cook, stirring occasionally, until all of their liquid is released, about 20 minutes. Add the broth and partially cover the pan. Cook over medium-low heat, stirring occasionally, until the eggplant is very soft and the mixture is very dry, about 1 hour. (Excess moisture can cause the filled pasta to crack when frozen.)

Allow the eggplant mixture to cool to room temperature, then grate the Taleggio into the mix. Add the parsley and toss to combine. (The filling can be made a day ahead of stuffing the pasta; store it, covered, in the fridge.)

FILL THE PASTA   Roll the dough into very thin sheets following the directions that came with your pasta machine or those on page 90. (You want the sheets thin enough so that you can see the shape of your hand through the pasta.) Line a sided baking sheet with parchment paper and flour the paper.

Very lightly brush some water over the entire pasta sheet. Place about a teaspoon of filling at 2-inch intervals just a little bit above the middle of the sheet. (You can use a pastry bag to do this if that's easier; just be sure the opening is big enough to accommodate the pieces of cheese in the filling.) Carefully lift the bottom edge of the sheet and bring it to meet the top, letting it fall loosely over the filling. Using the pinky side of each hand, gently pat the area close to each lump of filling to coax out any trapped air. Flour a 2-inch round pasta/pastry cutter and stamp out filled half-moons by positioning the cutter over each lump of filling so that the folded edge of the pasta is the diameter of the circle. As you work, transfer the filled pasta to the baking sheet in a single layer. (Don't stack them or they will stick together.) Freeze the pasta on the baking sheet until they feel rock solid, then transfer them to freezer bags or other airtight containers for longer storage. (They'll keep, frozen, for up to 2 weeks.) If you prefer to cook the pasta right away, freeze them for as long as you can so they will be easier to handle.

TO FINISH   Gently reheat the Cherry Tomato Sauce, if necessary. Bring a large pot of well-salted water to a boil. Reduce to a rapid simmer and cook the pasta until just tender. Meanwhile, heat the butter in a very large sauté pan over medium heat. Gently drain the pasta and add it to the pan with the butter. Increase the heat to medium-high and toss gently to coat. Sprinkle with grated cheese and about a teaspoon of the chives.

TO SERVE   Divide the pasta among warm bowls or plates. Top with a ladleful of the tomato sauce, some shavings of Parmigiano, and a tiny sprinkle of chives.

MEAT-FILLED AGNOLOTTI PLIN SERVES 4, WITH EXTRA PLIN TO FREEZE

When the *New York Times* asked me recently what I would choose as my last meal (kind of morbid, I know), I immediately said this pasta. The "sauce" for these purses of pasta is a simple one made from chicken broth and cheese. Tiny Honshimeji mushrooms have a delicious flavor, but I use them mainly because they look great on the plate. (Though shimeji are becoming more widely available, you can substitute diced button mushrooms if you can't find them.) This recipe will yield about 120 plin, enough for eight servings. Use only half the batch to feed four, and freeze the rest for future good eating. Or, double the sauce ingredients and feed eight people.

FOR THE FILLING

1 tablespoon extra virgin olive oil

1/4 pound skinless chicken leg meat, cut into 1 1/2- to 2-inch pieces

1/4 pound pork stew meat, such as shoulder, cut into 1-inch pieces

Kosher salt and freshly ground black pepper

3 shallots, sliced (1/2 cup)

1 quart Chicken Broth (page 241)

1 cup milk

1/2 pound fontina, cut into small cubes

1 tablespoon truffle oil

FOR THE PASTA AND SAUCE

Fresh Pasta Dough (page 88), rolled into thin sheets

3/4 cup grated Parmigiano-Reggiano, plus a couple inches of the cheese rind, if you have it

2 cups chicken broth

8 tablespoons (1 stick) unsalted butter, cut into pieces

2 teaspoons extra virgin olive oil

MAKE THE FILLING Heat the olive oil in a sauté pan over medium-high heat. Season the chicken and pork with salt and pepper and brown it on all sides. Add the shallots, cover with chicken broth by 1 inch, and bring to a boil. Lower the heat and simmer until the meat is thoroughly cooked, about 15 minutes. Strain the meat from the broth and reserve both. In a food processor, puree the meat, adding some of the reserved broth to make a very smooth mixture. Set aside.

Over a double boiler, heat the milk to a gentle simmer. Add the fontina in batches, stirring constantly with a whisk to make sure there are no lumps. The fondue is finished once the cheese has melted into the milk. (Occasionally, the fontina may separate; if it does, whisk it very briskly to bring it back together.)

Combine the meat and the cheese mixture. Add the truffle oil and season to taste with salt and pepper.

FILL THE PLIN Line a sided baking sheet with parchment paper and flour the paper. Cut a sheet of pasta so that its short side is about 3 inches and lightly brush it with water. Place dots of the filling, about a thimbleful, 1 inch apart along the middle of the strip. (Don't flatten

When you bite into these little tiny squares, you just have to sigh, the flavors are that good.

the filling; the finished plin should be about as tall as they are wide.) Fold the lower third of the strip up over the filling, without overlapping the top third of the strip. Fold the upper third down over the filling as if you were folding a letter. Using your fingers, gently pinch around each dot of filling to coax out any trapped air and seal the plin. Using a floured pasta/pastry cutter, cut between the dots of filling to make the individual plin. Repeat this process until you have used up all the filling; you should wind up with about 120 plin.

As you work, transfer the filled pasta to the baking sheet in a single layer. (Don't stack them or they will stick together.) Freeze the pasta on the baking sheet until they feel rock solid, then transfer them to freezer bags or other airtight containers and freeze for up to a month. (Freeze them in batches, as you will need only half of them for this recipe.) If you will cook the pasta soon, freeze them for as long as you can so they will be easier to handle.

MAKE THE SAUCE   If using the Parmigiano rind, simmer it with the chicken broth for 15 minutes, then remove it. If not, bring just the broth to a simmer. Whisk in about 6 tablespoons of the butter and ½ cup of the cheese. Cook this down until creamy, about 10 minutes. Keep warm.   *(continued)*

1 medium carrot, very finely diced (about ½ cup)

1 cup Honshimeji mushroom caps (plus a bit of stem), left whole if tiny or cut in half

1 teaspoon diced preserved truffles (optional)

1½ tablespoons chopped fresh chives

COOK THE VEGETABLES AND PASTA   Bring a large pot of well-salted water to a boil. Heat the olive oil in a large sauté pan (the pasta will be added to this pan) over medium heat. Add the carrot and mushrooms and cook, stirring, until just tender but not browned. Add *half* of the frozen plin to the boiling water and cook until tender and hot throughout (taste one to see), 5 to 7 minutes. Reserve a cup of the pasta water and drain the pasta. Add the pasta, the remaining 2 tablespoons of butter, the preserved truffles, if using, and ½ cup of the reserved pasta water to the pan with the carrot and mushrooms and toss together over medium-low heat.

TO SERVE   Use a hand blender to quickly whisk the sauce or whisk it vigorously by hand. Divide the pasta among warm serving bowls. Top each with a large dollop of the sauce, sprinkle with the remaining cheese, and garnish with the chives. Serve immediately.

ORECCHIETTE WITH GREEN BEANS, POTATOES, AND BASIL SERVES 3 TO 4

This summery recipe is based on a Ligurian tradition of cooking potatoes and pasta together; the starch from the potato clings to the pasta, making the sauce adhere better still. To keep the puree's bright green color, chill the olive oil for about half an hour before blending it with the basil.

1/2 cup extra virgin olive oil

2 cups fresh basil leaves

Kosher salt

3 1/2 ounces green beans (about 24), cut diagonally into 1-inch pieces (2/3 cup)

4 medium fingerling potatoes, diced (1 2/3 cups)

1/2 pound fresh or dried orecchiette

Freshly ground black pepper

2/3 cup fresh ricotta

1/4 cup toasted chopped hazelnuts

1/4 cup grated pecorino Romano

MAKE THE BASIL PUREE   Combine the olive oil, basil leaves, and 1/2 teaspoon salt in a blender and puree until smooth. (You can make this a day ahead and refrigerate it, though it might darken.)

COOK THE VEGETABLES AND PASTA   Bring a pot of well-salted water to a boil. Add the beans and cook until just tender, 4 or 5 minutes. Remove with a slotted spoon and reserve. Add the potatoes to the pot and cook them until just tender, about 7 minutes. Remove with a slotted spoon. Add the orecchiette to the pot and cook until al dente. Reserve 1 cup of the pasta water, drain the pasta, then return it to the pot. Add the green beans and potatoes, season amply with pepper and a little salt, and toss well. If the mixture looks very dry, add a little of the pasta water.

TO SERVE   Divide the pasta among warm bowls and top each with a large dollop of ricotta. Drizzle the puree over the top. Sprinkle with the hazelnuts and pecorino, season with additional salt and pepper if needed, and serve immediately.

CANNELLINI BEAN AND SAUSAGE LASAGNA SERVES 6 TO 8

A flavorful bean puree takes the place of the tomato sauce in this luscious, rosemary-scented sausage lasagna. I prefer a lasagna with many thin layers and so recommend a light hand as you add each ingredient. But I also don't think people should get as hung up as they do when making lasagna. The order of ingredients, for example, does not have to stay the same with each layer. You can even leave an ingredient out of a layer and the world won't end. If you run out of sausage but still have more beans, then make a layer of just beans. There is really no right or wrong way to layer lasagna, which is why I don't tell you how many layers to strive for or even which to end with, because it's all good.

MAKE THE BEAN PUREE Heat 2 tablespoons of the olive oil in a soup pot over medium heat. Add the onion and cook, stirring occasionally, until just tender, about 7 minutes. Add the garlic and 2 rosemary sprigs, and cook, stirring, another 2 to 3 minutes. Drain the beans and add them to the soup pot along with the chicken broth. Bring to a boil, then lower to a simmer and cook, uncovered, until the beans are pleasantly tender, about 1 hour (sometimes longer, depending on the beans); taste a bean to determine tenderness.

Drain the beans, reserving the cooking liquid. Set aside 2 cups of the cooked beans. Puree the remaining beans (remove the rosemary sprigs first) in a blender or food processor with as much cooking liquid as necessary (1 to 1¼ cups) to create a texture similar to that of fresh ricotta. As you puree the beans, add another 2 tablespoons of olive oil. Season to taste with salt and pepper. (The puree can be made a day or two before assembling the pasta.)

MAKE THE ROSEMARY OIL In a small saucepan, simmer the remaining ¼ cup of olive oil with the remaining 2 rosemary sprigs for 10 minutes. Take off the heat and let sit to further infuse the flavor. (You can make the oil up to 5 days ahead as long as you keep it refrigerated.)

$^1/_2$ cup extra virgin olive oil, plus more as needed

1 medium onion, chopped

2 garlic cloves, chopped

4 small fresh rosemary sprigs

1 pound dried white beans, such as cannellini, soaked in water for at least 8 hours

3 quarts Chicken Broth (page 241)

Kosher salt and freshly ground black pepper

$^1/_2$ pound sweet Italian sausage

$^1/_2$ pound spicy Italian sausage

1 cup diced tomato

Fresh Pasta Dough (page 88), rolled into thin sheets, or purchased fresh pasta sheets, cooked until just barely al dente and well drained (see page 94)

$^1/_2$ pound fresh mozzarella, grated or cut into small cubes

1 cup grated Parmigiano-Reggiano, plus more if needed

1 small bunch fresh parsley, finely chopped

COOK THE SAUSAGE   Heat a large sauté pan over medium-high heat. Remove the sausage from its casing and cook, adjusting the heat as needed, until the sausage is completely cooked through. Use a wooden spoon to break it into small pieces and add a little oil if necessary. Toss the tomato with the sausage and reserve off the heat.

ASSEMBLE AND BAKE THE LASAGNA   Heat the oven to 300°F. Spread a thin layer of the pureed beans on the bottom of a 9 by 13-inch baking pan. Add some cooked pasta sheets next, overlapping them slightly. Top with a thin layer of the pureed beans and drizzle about 1 teaspoon of the rosemary oil over them. Then scatter some of the whole beans, sausage, mozzarella, Parmigiano, and parsley evenly over the pureed beans. Make another layer of pasta sheets and top it with more bean puree, rosemary oil, whole beans, sausage, mozzarella, and light sprinklings of Parmigiano and parsley. Continue layering, making as many thin layers as possible, until you run out of ingredients or the lasagna rises ¼ inch above the pan, whichever comes first. End with whichever layer you're on at that point and give it a final sprinkling of Parmigiano.

Bake until hot throughout, 50 minutes to 1 hour. Let the lasagna rest for 10 minutes before slicing and serving.

RISOTTO SERVES 4

This risotto is the foundation for most of my flavored variations. It makes a wonderful side dish as is, but I hope you will also use it as a springboard for your own risotto toppings and additions. If your addition is very quick cooking, such as chopped shrimp or spinach, you need only to add it raw toward the end of cooking. Anything that might take longer should first be parcooked. Made with the broth on page 241, this simplest of risottos is something special.

TOAST THE RICE   In a wide, heavy-based saucepan, heat about 3 tablespoons of the olive oil over medium-high heat until very hot. Add the shallot and red pepper flakes and stir until the shallot is barely browned, about 2 minutes. Add the rice and cook, stirring with long strokes, until each grain is coated with oil, another 1 to 2 minutes. Pour in about ¼ cup of the wine and boil until it is almost completely absorbed. Do not let the pot become completely dry; a little liquid should remain on top of the rice.

MAKE THE RISOTTO   Add a couple ladlefuls of the hot broth to the rice and stir well every minute or so until almost all of the liquid has been absorbed. (On medium-high heat, the risotto bubbles away throughout, which is fine.) To test whether to add more liquid, drag the spoon through the rice; if the liquid doesn't immediately fill in the space, it's time to add more. Add another ladleful of broth, the remaining wine, and about a tablespoon of olive oil. Continue to cook, adding more broth as needed and stirring, until the risotto is al dente, 20 to 25 minutes. If the risotto seems too dry, add a bit more broth. If there's too much broth in the pan, but the rice is done, crank up the heat to evaporate the liquid. Bear in mind that the risotto will thicken a bit as you add the cheese and it cools.

TO SERVE   Remove the rice from heat. Add a final drizzle of olive oil, the butter, and the cheese, and stir until well combined and cohesive. Season to taste with salt, if needed (it might not be, if you used purchased broth). Serve immediately.

4 to 5 tablespoons extra virgin olive oil

1 small shallot, finely chopped (about 1 tablespoon)

Pinch of crushed red pepper flakes

1 cup Vialone Nano or Arborio rice

1/2 cup dry white wine, such as Sauvignon Blanc

1 quart Chicken Broth (page 241), kept at a simmer

1 tablespoon unsalted butter

2 tablespoons grated Parmigiano-Reggiano

Kosher salt

BRAISED OXTAIL AND SWEET POTATO RISOTTO SERVES 6

Bony oxtail does not yield a lot of meat, but what it does is incredibly full flavored and perfect as part of a hearty sauce for a fall-inspired risotto.

4 pounds oxtails

Kosher salt and freshly ground black pepper

2 tablespoons extra virgin olive oil, plus more as needed

1 small carrot, finely diced

1 celery stalk, finely diced

1 medium onion, chopped

4 garlic cloves, coarsely chopped

3/4 cup red wine

1/2 cup red wine vinegar

6 plum tomatoes, quartered and seeded

2 cups Chicken Reduction (page 242) or good-quality purchased chicken base, reconstituted as the package directs until a little thicker than chicken broth

3 small fresh thyme sprigs

3 small fresh rosemary sprigs

Sweet Potato Risotto (recipe follows)

1 tablespoon freshly grated horseradish

Sea salt

BROWN THE OXTAILS   Heat the oven to 300°F. Season the oxtails all over with salt and pepper. Heat the olive oil in a deep, heavy-based Dutch oven or similar pot over medium-high heat. Sear the oxtails—in two batches if they don't fit in the pot in a single layer—until they are well browned all over.

MAKE THE SAUCE AND BRAISE THE OXTAILS   Remove the oxtails and add the carrot, celery, onion, and garlic along with more olive oil, if necessary. Cook, stirring, until the vegetables are browned, 3 to 4 minutes. Add the wine and vinegar to the pan and, using a wooden spoon, scrape up the bits stuck to the bottom. Continue to cook until the liquid is reduced by about one-third. Add the tomatoes, the chicken reduction, and the thyme and rosemary. Return the oxtails to the pot, bring the liquid to a boil, cover, and put in the oven. Cook, turning the oxtails occasionally, until the meat is just barely clinging to the bone, about 3 hours.

Remove the oxtails from the sauce and strain, reserving the cooking liquid. When the oxtails are cool enough to handle, remove as much meat as you can from the bones. (You can braise the oxtails up to a couple days ahead. Pour a little of the braising liquid over the meat and then refrigerate each separately. Once the braising liquid is cold, you can easily remove the hardened layer of fat.) If using right away, use a large spoon or ladle to remove as much as possible of the clear fat floating on top of the braising liquid. Heat over medium-high heat until reduced by about a quarter and slightly thickened.

TO SERVE   Add the meat to the sauce and reheat gently. Divide the Sweet Potato Risotto among six wide, shallow bowls. Use a slotted spoon to portion some of the oxtail meat over each bowl. Pour a large spoonful of the sauce over the meat. Garnish each bowl with some freshly grated horseradish and a tiny pinch of sea salt and serve immediately.

SWEET POTATO RISOTTO

SERVES 6

Delicious with the oxtail, this pretty risotto also makes a wonderful side dish or middle course on its own.

5 to 6 tablespoons extra virgin olive oil

1 small fresh thyme sprig

1 medium sweet potato, peeled and cut into a small dice

1 quart Chicken Broth (page 241), kept at a simmer

1 small shallot, finely chopped (about 1 tablespoon)

Pinch of crushed red pepper flakes

1 cup Vialone Nano or Arborio rice

$^1/_2$ cup dry white wine, such as Sauvignon Blanc

1 tablespoon unsalted butter

2 tablespoons grated Parmigiano-Reggiano

Kosher salt

SAUTÉ THE SWEET POTATO   In a medium sauté pan, heat 1 tablespoon of the olive oil over medium-high heat. Add the thyme and sweet potato and cook, stirring occasionally, until the potato is lightly browned. Add a couple tablespoons of the chicken broth to

the pan, reduce the heat to medium-low, and cook until the potato is just tender, 4 to 5 minutes. Remove from the heat and reserve.

MAKE THE RISOTTO   In a wide, heavy-based saucepan, heat about 3 tablespoons of the olive oil over medium-high heat until very hot. Add the shallot and red pepper flakes and stir until the shallot is barely browned, about 2 minutes. (Take the pan off the heat if the shallot starts to scorch.) Add the rice and cook, stirring with long strokes, until each grain is coated with oil, another 1 to 2 minutes. Pour in about ¼ cup of the wine and boil until it is almost completely absorbed. Do not let the pot become completely dry; a little liquid should remain on top of the rice.

Add a couple ladlefuls of the hot broth to the rice and stir well every minute or so until almost all of the liquid has been absorbed. (On medium-high heat, the risotto bubbles away throughout, which is fine.) To test whether to add more liquid, drag the spoon through the rice; if the liquid doesn't immediately fill in the space, it's time to add more. Add another ladleful of broth, the remaining wine, and about a tablespoon of olive oil. Continue to cook, adding more broth as needed and stirring, until the risotto is al dente, 20 to 25 minutes. Add the sweet potato (remove the thyme sprig) and stir.

If the risotto seems too dry, add a bit more broth. If there's too much broth in the pan, but the rice is done, crank up the heat to evaporate the liquid. Bear in mind that the risotto will thicken a bit as you add the cheese and it cools.

TO SERVE   Remove the rice from heat and let stand for about 30 seconds. Add a final drizzle of olive oil, the butter, and the cheese, and stir with a wooden spoon until well combined and cohesive. Season to taste with salt, if needed (it might not be, if you used purchased broth). Serve on its own or topped with braised oxtail (preceding recipe).

FAVA BEAN RISOTTO WITH MORELS, PECORINO, AND BALSAMIC VINEGAR SERVES 4

Morels and fava beans are a classic combination and one that heralds spring, a season of excitement for a chef.

PUREE THE FAVA BEANS Bring a small saucepan of salted water to a boil. Add the favas and cook until tender, 3 to 4 minutes. Drain, cool slightly, and pinch off their tough skins. Reserve half the beans and puree the rest, adding a tablespoon or two of chicken broth, if needed.

SEAR THE MORELS Heat a couple teaspoons of the olive oil in a small sauté pan over medium-high heat. Add the morels and cook until tender, about 5 minutes. Toss in the chives, remove from heat, and reserve.

MAKE THE RISOTTO In a wide, heavy-based saucepan, heat about 3 tablespoons of the olive oil over medium-high heat until very hot. Add the shallot and red pepper flakes and stir until the shallot is barely browned, about 2 minutes. (Take the pan off the heat if the shallot starts to scorch.) Add the rice and cook, stirring with long strokes, until each grain is coated with oil, another 1 to 2 minutes. Pour in about ¼ cup of the wine and boil until it is almost completely absorbed. Do not let the pot become completely dry; a little liquid should remain on top of the rice.

Add a couple ladlefuls of the hot broth to the rice and stir well every minute or so until almost all of the liquid has been absorbed. (On medium-high heat, the risotto bubbles away throughout, which is fine.) To test whether to add more liquid, drag the spoon through the rice; if the liquid doesn't immediately fill in the space, it's time to add more. Add another ladleful of broth, the remaining wine, and about a tablespoon of olive oil. Continue to cook, adding more

Kosher salt

1 cup fava beans

4 to 4^1/$_2$ cups Chicken Broth (page 241), kept at a simmer

5 to 6 tablespoons extra virgin olive oil

^{1}/$_4$ pound fresh morel mushrooms, cleaned and quartered

1 teaspoon chopped fresh chives

1 small shallot, finely chopped (about 1 tablespoon)

Pinch of crushed red pepper flakes

1 cup Vialone Nano or Arborio rice

^{1}/$_2$ cup dry white wine, such as Sauvignon Blanc

1 tablespoon unsalted butter

2 tablespoons grated pecorino Romano

1 tablespoon aged balsamic vinegar

broth as needed and stirring, until the risotto looks creamy and the grains are cooked through but pleasantly al dente, 20 to 25 minutes.

Stir in the fava bean puree and the reserved beans and cook until heated through. If the risotto seems too dry, add a bit more broth. If there's too much broth in the pan, but the rice is done, crank up the heat to evaporate the liquid. Bear in mind that the risotto will thicken a bit as you add the cheese and it cools.

TO SERVE   Reheat the mushrooms if necessary. Remove the rice from heat and let stand for about 30 seconds. Add a final drizzle of olive oil, the butter, and 1 tablespoon of the cheese, and stir with a wooden spoon until well combined and cohesive. Divide the risotto among warm serving bowls and spoon the mushrooms on top. Finish each serving with a drizzle of the vinegar and a sprinkle of cheese.

ROCK SHRIMP RISOTTO WITH SPRING VEGETABLES AND CRISPY SHALLOTS SERVES 4

Delicious on its own, this bright risotto tastes even better with the warm, sweet flavor and crisp texture of easy-to-make fried shallots.

MAKE THE RISOTTO   In a wide, heavy-based saucepan, heat about 3 tablespoons of the olive oil over medium-high heat until very hot. Add the shallot and red pepper flakes and stir until the shallot is barely browned, about 2 minutes. (Take the pan off the heat if the shallot starts to scorch.) Add the rice and cook over medium-high heat, stirring with long strokes, until each grain is coated with oil, another 1 to 2 minutes. Pour in about ¼ cup of the wine and boil until it is almost completely absorbed. Do not let the pot become completely dry; a little liquid should remain on top of the rice.

Add a couple ladlefuls of the hot broth to the rice and stir well every minute or so until almost all of the liquid has been absorbed. (On medium-high heat, the risotto bubbles away throughout, which is fine.) To test whether to add more liquid, drag the spoon through the rice; if the liquid doesn't immediately fill in the space, it's time to add more. Add another ladleful of broth, the remaining wine, and about a tablespoon of olive oil. Continue cooking, stirring and adding more broth as needed, until the rice is al dente, about 20 minutes. Add the peas, asparagus, scallions, and shrimp, plus a little additional broth if the mixture looks dry; cook until the shrimp are just cooked through and the vegetables are tender, another 5 minutes.

TO SERVE   Remove the rice from heat and let stand for about 30 seconds. Add a final drizzle of olive oil and the butter and stir with a wooden spoon until well combined and cohesive. Season to taste with salt, if needed. Divide the risotto among warm bowls and serve immediately, topped with about a tablespoon of crispy shallots.

(continued)

4 to 5 tablespoons extra virgin olive oil

1 small shallot, finely chopped (about 1 tablespoon)

Pinch of crushed red pepper flakes

1 cup Vialone Nano or Arborio rice

½ cup dry white wine, such as Sauvignon Blanc

1 quart Chicken Broth (page 241), kept at a simmer

½ cup fresh or defrosted frozen peas

½ cup very thinly sliced asparagus

¼ cup very thinly sliced scallions

1 cup rock shrimp, well rinsed, or 1 cup peeled, deveined, and coarsely chopped medium shrimp

1 tablespoon unsalted butter

Kosher salt

Crispy Shallots (recipe follows)

CRISPY SHALLOTS

MAKES ABOUT $^1/_2$ CUP

These fried shallots make a lively, fun, and delicious garnish for all kinds of dishes, including pureed soups, salads, and, of course, risotto. Whenever I am making some for a specific dish, I always make a little extra because I can't help nibbling on them. Once drained and cooled, they'll keep in an airtight container for at least a week, so consider doubling or even tripling this batch.

$^1/_4$ cup extra virgin olive oil, plus more if needed
2 shallots, thinly sliced
Kosher salt

Heat the oil in a medium sauté pan over medium heat. Add the shallots and cook, stirring occasionally, until the pieces begin to color, then stirring more often to brown them evenly all over, 12 to 15 minutes. Don't be tempted to rush them by increasing the heat or they won't be as sweet or as crispy. Drain the shallots in a single layer on paper towels. Season with a little salt while still hot.

Sweet, sumptuous lobster snuggles right into a bed of risotto for a dish that's as soothing as it is extravagant.

LOBSTER RISOTTO SERVES 4

For an even more pronounced lobster flavor, use lobster broth in place of chicken broth (save lobster shells to make the simple one on page 244). Sautéed mushrooms and butternut squash would also be delicious in place of the peas and asparagus.

PARCOOK THE LOBSTER   Bring to a boil a pot of salted water large enough to hold the lobster. Put the lobster in head first, cover, and cook for 4 minutes. You're not cooking the lobster fully at this point; it will finish cooking in the risotto. Remove the lobster from the pot. When cool enough to handle, remove the meat from the large lobster claws and the tail. Cut the tail lengthwise and remove the intestinal tract. (You can do this up to a day ahead; wrap the lobster meat in plastic and refrigerate.) Rinse the shells and use them to make the lobster broth, if you like.

MAKE THE RISOTTO   In a wide, heavy-based saucepan, heat about 3 tablespoons of the olive oil over medium-high heat until very hot. Add the shallot and red pepper flakes and stir until the shallot turns light golden, about 2 minutes. (Take the pan off the heat if the shallot starts to scorch.) Add the rice and cook, stirring with long strokes, until each grain is coated with oil, another 1 to 2 minutes. Pour in about ¼ cup of the wine and boil until it is almost completely absorbed. Do not let the pot become completely dry; a little liquid should remain on top of the rice.   *(continued)*

Kosher salt

1 lobster, $1^1/_4$ to $1^1/_2$ pounds

4 to 5 tablespoons extra virgin olive oil

1 small shallot, finely chopped (about 1 tablespoon)

Pinch of crushed red pepper flakes

1 cup Vialone Nano or Arborio rice

$^1/_2$ cup dry white wine, such as Sauvignon Blanc

1 quart Chicken Broth (page 241) or Lobster Broth (page 244), kept at a simmer

1 tablespoon unsalted butter at room temperature

$^1/_2$ cup frozen peas, blanched

$^1/_2$ cup very thinly sliced asparagus (from about 8 stalks), blanched

1 small leek, white and light green parts, cut into a medium dice and blanched

$^1/_2$ teaspoon Chile Oil (page 27) or storebought (optional)

Add a couple ladlefuls of the hot broth to the rice and stir well every minute or so until almost all of the liquid has been absorbed. (On medium-high heat, the risotto bubbles away throughout, which is fine.) To test whether to add more liquid, drag the spoon through the rice; if the liquid doesn't immediately fill in the space, it's time to add more. Add another ladleful of broth, the remaining wine, and about a tablespoon of olive oil. Continue to cook, adding more broth as needed and stirring, until the risotto looks creamy but is still al dente, about 20 minutes. If the risotto seems too dry, add a bit more broth. If there's too much broth in the pan, but the rice is done, crank up the heat to evaporate the liquid. Bear in mind that the risotto will thicken a bit as it cools.

TO SERVE   Chop the lobster meat into pieces small enough to eat comfortably without a knife yet large enough to make its presence known. Remove the rice from heat and let stand for about 30 seconds. Add the lobster, butter, peas, asparagus, leek, and a drizzle of olive oil (or the chile oil, if you prefer). Stir with a wooden spoon until well combined. Season to taste with salt, if needed (it might not be, if you used purchased broth). Serve immediately.

CHICKEN LIVER AND SPINACH RISOTTO SERVES 6

A glass of red wine, a bright green salad, and this rustic risotto—it's all good. Spinach not only tastes good in this dish but is also easy to add at the last minute with minimal preparation. If you'd like a heartier green to go with the full-flavored liver, substitute blanched Swiss chard or broccoli rabe for the spinach.

PREPARE THE LIVERS   In a small sauté pan, heat 1½ teaspoons of the olive oil over medium heat. Add the sliced shallots and a pinch of salt and cook, stirring occasionally, until quite brown, about 10 minutes. Combine the shallots, chicken livers, and 1 teaspoon of salt and mix well.

MAKE THE RISOTTO   In a wide, heavy-based saucepan, heat about 3 tablespoons of the olive oil over medium-high heat until very hot. Add the chopped shallot and the red pepper flakes and stir until the shallot is barely browned, about 2 minutes. (Take the pan off the heat if the shallot starts to scorch.) Add the rice and cook over medium-high heat, stirring with long strokes, until each grain is coated with oil, another 1 to 2 minutes. Pour in about ¼ cup of the wine and boil until it is almost completely absorbed. Do not let the pot become completely dry; a little liquid should remain on top of the rice.

Add a couple ladlefuls of the hot broth to the rice and stir well every minute or so until almost all of the liquid has been absorbed. (On medium-high heat, the risotto bubbles away throughout, which is fine.) To test whether to add more liquid, drag the spoon through the rice; if the liquid doesn't immediately fill in the space, it's time to add more. Add another ladleful of broth, the remaining wine, and about a tablespoon of olive oil. Continue to cook, adding more broth as needed and stirring, until the risotto looks creamy but is still al dente, 20 to 25 minutes. *(continued)*

6 tablespoons extra virgin olive oil

¼ cup thinly sliced shallots plus
   1 tablespoon finely chopped shallot
   (2 large or 3 medium shallots)

Kosher salt

1 cup trimmed chicken livers, finely
   chopped

Pinch of crushed red pepper flakes

1 cup Vialone Nano or Arborio rice

½ cup dry white wine, such as
   Sauvignon Blanc

1 quart Chicken Broth (page 241), kept at
   a simmer

½ cup coarsely chopped fresh spinach,
   well washed and dried

1 tablespoon unsalted butter

2 tablespoons grated Parmigiano-
   Reggiano

2 teaspoons chopped fresh chives

A couple minutes before serving, add the chicken livers and stir well. Add the spinach and stir to wilt it. If the risotto seems too dry, add a bit more broth. If there's too much broth in the pan but the rice is done, crank up the heat to evaporate the liquid. Bear in mind that the risotto will thicken a bit as you add the cheese and it cools.

TO SERVE   Remove the rice from heat and let stand for about 30 seconds. Add a final drizzle of olive oil, the butter, cheese, and chives, and stir with a wooden spoon until well combined and cohesive. Season to taste with salt and serve immediately.

POTATO GNOCCHI WITH FRESH TOMATO SAUCE

SERVES 6; MAKES ABOUT 7 CUPS OF GNOCCHI

If you can make a snake out of Play-Doh, you can make my gnocchi. That's because instead of rolling each piece off a fork or a gnocchi board to give it grooves, I simply roll out a piece of dough and cut it into pieces. I prefer the smoother texture of gnocchi made this way, but I also don't mind the fact that this method is much less tedious. As with freshly made pasta, I think gnocchi only benefits from a deep freeze; the little dumplings absorb less water during cooking and turn out meltingly tender yet sturdy enough to toss in your sauce without the risk of becoming a heap of mush. For the best texture, use a ricer to mash the potatoes.

BOIL THE POTATOES   Put the potatoes, whole and unpeeled, in a large pot of salted water. Bring to a boil and cook until just tender when pierced with a paring knife, 30 to 35 minutes; do not overcook. Drain the potatoes, rice them into a bowl, and let cool to room temperature.

MAKE THE GNOCCHI DOUGH   Add ¼ cup of the Parmigiano, the egg, egg yolk, and teaspoon of salt to the potatoes and mix well. Generously flour your work surface. Dump the potatoes out and lightly knead in about 1 cup of the flour. Gradually add more flour until the mixture just begins to hold together and feels soft and supple. Shape and freeze the dough right away; if gnocchi dough sits too long it becomes impossible to roll.

SHAPE THE GNOCCHI   Line a sided baking sheet (one that will fit in your freezer) with parchment paper and lightly flour it. Using light pressure so as not to squash the delicate dough, roll the dough into ropes about ½ inch thick. Using a sharp knife, cut each rope on a diagonal at intervals of about ½ inch. Transfer the gnocchi to the prepared baking sheet in one layer and freeze. When they're rock hard, transfer them to zip-top freezer bags or other airtight containers for longer storage.

(continued)

2 pounds Yukon gold potatoes (about 4 large)

1 teaspoon kosher salt, plus more for cooking

¾ cup grated Parmigiano-Reggiano

1 large egg

1 large egg yolk

1½ to 2 cups "00" or all-purpose flour, plus more for rolling and shaping

Fresh Tomato Sauce (recipe follows)

1 tablespoon unsalted butter

2 teaspoons finely chopped fresh chives (optional)

TO SERVE   Bring a large pot of well-salted water to a boil. Reheat the tomato sauce in a large sauté pan, if necessary. Boil the gnocchi until they are tender with no raw flour taste, usually 1 to 2 minutes after they begin to float. Drain the gnocchi. Over medium heat, toss the gnocchi with the tomato sauce, the butter, and most of the remaining ½ cup of cheese. Divide the gnocchi among warm serving bowls. Finish with a sprinkling of cheese and the chives, if using.

FRESH TOMATO SAUCE
MAKES ABOUT 3 CUPS; SERVES 4 TO 6

This tomato sauce on top of potato gnocchi is pure comfort food. It's also wonderful tossed with spaghetti and finished with a little butter, a little Parmigiano, and fresh basil. Consider doubling the recipe and freezing the leftover in various amounts; with its pure tomato flavor, this is the sauce I use in all my recipes that call for tomato sauce.

$\frac{1}{3}$ cup extra virgin olive oil

20 plum tomatoes, peeled, seeded, and coarsely chopped

Pinch of crushed red pepper flakes

Kosher salt and freshly ground black pepper

In a large sauté pan, heat the ⅓ cup of olive oil over medium-high heat until quite hot. Add the tomatoes and red pepper flakes, and season lightly with salt and pepper. Let the tomatoes cook for a few minutes to soften. Then, using a potato masher, crush the tomatoes. Cook for 20 to 25 minutes, until the tomatoes are tender and the sauce has thickened. If using right away for the gnocchi, leave the sauce in the pan; otherwise, refrigerate the sauce for up to 2 days or freeze it.

CHICKEN-FILLED GNOCCHI DUMPLINGS WITH LENTIL SAUCE

SERVES 8 AS A FIRST COURSE, 4 AS A MAIN COURSE; MAKES ABOUT 50 DUMPLINGS

The filling for this recipe begins with aromatic braised chicken. Enjoy the chicken itself one night as a dinner for two, then make the gnocchi dumplings with the leftovers the next day. Don't worry about chicken overkill; you can make the dumplings and freeze them for up to a month; in fact, they'll cook up better after being frozen. However, you can't make the gnocchi dough ahead of stuffing it, or the dough will become too wet to handle.

MAKE THE FILLING   Chop the chicken pieces coarsely and put them in a food processor. Add ½ cup of the braising liquid and the Parmigiano-Reggiano and pulse to puree into a mousselike texture, adding additional braising liquid if needed. Chill the filling to firm it a bit.

FILL THE DUMPLINGS   Roll the gnocchi dough on a lightly floured surface to a thickness of about ¼ inch. Using a 2-inch cookie cutter, cut rounds from the dough. Because the dough rounds will spring back a little and thicken slightly, it's best to press each circle gently with your fingertips to thin it and increase its area; otherwise you will need to use less filling. Line a sided baking sheet (one that will fit in your freezer) with parchment paper and lightly flour it.

Taste the filling and season with additional salt; you want it to be highly seasoned. Put a scant teaspoon of filling toward the middle of each circle, fold the dough over to a half moon, and press the edges to seal. Freeze the dumplings in a single layer on the prepared baking sheet; when rock hard, they can be transferred to an airtight container.

COOK THE LENTILS   Put the lentils in a medium saucepan with water to cover by 2 inches. Add the 2 teaspoons of kosher salt and bring to a boil. Reduce to a simmer and cook until the lentils are tender but hold their shape, about 25 minutes. Drain.

½ recipe Rustic Braised Chicken (page 164), including ¾ cup of the braising liquid, made to the point of serving, then cooled

1 tablespoon finely grated Parmigiano-Reggiano, plus more for serving

Gnocchi Dough (recipe follows)

All-purpose flour for dusting

2 teaspoons kosher salt, plus more for seasoning

1 cup French green lentils (lentils du Puy)

2 tablespoons extra virgin olive oil

2 shallots, finely chopped

½ cup very finely diced carrot

½ cup good-quality tomato puree

1 tablespoon finely chopped preserved black truffles (optional)

2 tablespoons chopped fresh parsley

2 teaspoons chopped fresh chives, plus more for serving (optional)

1 to 2 teaspoons truffle oil

MAKE THE SAUCE   In a medium sauté pan, heat the olive oil over medium-high heat. Add the shallots and carrot and cook, stirring, until tender and light golden, about 5 minutes. Add the lentils, the tomato puree, the preserved truffles, if using, the parsley, and the chives. Cook for a few minutes, stirring, then reserve off the heat. (You can make this "sauce" ahead and refrigerate it for a day or so; reheat it before serving.)

TO FINISH   Bring a large pot of well-salted water to a boil. Cook the dumplings at a gentle boil until the filling is cooked through, about 5 minutes. Carefully drain. Meanwhile, reheat the lentil sauce. Divide it among shallow serving bowls and top with six or so of the dumplings for a first course, more for an entrée. Drizzle each with a little truffle oil and sprinkle with a bit more Parmigiano and chives, if you like.

GNOCCHI DOUGH

MAKES ENOUGH DOUGH FOR 50 DUMPLINGS

For the best texture, you'll need a ricer to mash the potatoes.

2 pounds Yukon gold potatoes (about 4 large)

1 teaspoon kosher salt, plus more for cooking

1 large egg

1 large egg yolk

1^1/$_2$ to 2 cups "00" or all-purpose flour, plus more
    for rolling and shaping

^{1}/$_4$ cup finely grated grana Padano or
    Parmigiano-Reggiano (optional)

BOIL THE POTATOES   Put the potatoes, whole and unpeeled, in a medium pot of well-salted water. Bring to a boil and cook until just tender when pierced with a paring knife, 30 to 35 minutes. Do not overcook the potatoes; they should still hold their shape. Drain the potatoes, rice them into a bowl, and let cool to room temperature.

MAKE THE DOUGH   Add the egg, egg yolk, and teaspoon of salt to the potatoes and mix well. Generously flour your work surface. Dump the potatoes out with the grated cheese, if using, and lightly knead in about 1 cup of the flour. Gradually add more flour until the mixture just begins to hold together and feels soft and supple. Don't be tempted to add too much flour at once; you can always add more if the dough needs it. Use the dough right away; it does not hold well.

Main Courses

When I create main-course dishes, I consider the whole plate, which is why most of the main dishes in this book include accompaniments tailor-made for them. But I am not a tyrant, so unless the accompaniment is completely integrated into the main course, such as the tomatoes served with the whole red snapper (page 148), you can easily choose to serve the main course with something else entirely (though, of course, I like to think my way is best). This is why I have the "sides" running near the main course for which they were designed but have kept them as distinct recipes. Most of these side dishes—Sautéed Broccoli Rabe (page 169), Minted Couscous (page 198), and Concentrated Tomatoes (page 135)—are so easy and versatile that you will want to include them in your everyday cooking repertoire. (For a list of all the side dishes scattered throughout the book, look under side dishes in the index.)

In my restaurants, these side dishes really act more like garnishes. My hope is that by the time you come to the protein part of the meal, you have already enjoyed a starter as well as a pasta course. Therefore the actual main course is on the smaller side, as is the accompaniment. I understand that's not how most people eat at home, so as these recipes were tested, the amount of, say, couscous, potatoes, or kale was upped to a more conventional side-dish portion.

FISH

I love to visit the Adriatic coast of Italy in no small part because of the phenomenal fish dishes I've enjoyed in that beautiful part of the world. When I return home, I try to re-create that excitement by creating inspired fish recipes, many of which I have included in this chapter. Featuring fish so dominantly is a bit of a risk because although I know it's a favorite to order out, most people tend not to cook much fish at home. If you think about it, this doesn't make much sense, since fish is so tasty, so good for us, and so quick to cook. I believe two hurdles get in the way for home cooks: a lack of access to good-quality fish and a lack of experience cooking it.

The issue of quality is important, but better and better fish appear on the market every day. One thing to keep in mind is that with fish, "fresh" does not always mean high quality. You are often much better off buying, say, swordfish that was frozen at sea (and kept frozen) than fish that was frozen and then thawed for the display case. (Of course, the very best fish is that caught the same day you buy it, something you can enjoy if you live near the coast.) Also, try to patronize a fish market with a knowledgeable person behind the counter; he or she can direct you to the fish that would make the best substitute if the one called for in a recipe is unavailable or of lesser quality. On that note, buying fish can be confusing because the same (or very similar) fish can go by different names depending on where it was caught. For the recipes that feature a fish species that may not be as widely available, I offer a more common substitute. As you get to know the different textures of the fish—flaky, meaty, oily, steaklike—you can choose the fish you think is best suited to the dish.

Finally, I would like to pretend that we chefs are the only ones who can cook fish to perfection. But with a little experience, anybody can. One trick for cooking flakier fish so it's perfectly golden on the outside and tender within is to use a good amount of oil and get the pan very hot. Slide the fish in and let it sit, undisturbed, until its underside has a crisp, dark crust. Use a flexible spatula to turn the fish over without lifting it completely from the oil. Lift up one edge of the fish and let it gently fall back into the oil on its uncooked side as if you were turning a page in a book. This little move helps keep flaky fish from coming apart during cooking. Finally, turn off the heat before you think the fish is fully cooked and let the residual heat from the pan finish cooking it to tender perfection. Getting the timing right will take some experience, but pay attention to how the fish looks and feels when it's cooked to your liking, then use that information the next time you cook the same kind of fish.

GRILLED SWORDFISH WITH OLIVES AND TOMATOES   SERVES 4

This dish is quick, simple, and pretty. What more could you ask?

3 plum tomatoes

2 to 3 tablespoons extra virgin olive oil

1 cup cherry tomatoes, cut in half

Kosher salt

12 black olives, such as Gaeta, finely chopped (about 2 tablespoons)

1¹/₂ teaspoons finely chopped fresh oregano

1¹/₂ teaspoons finely chopped fresh basil

1¹/₂ teaspoons red wine vinegar

1 small bunch watercress, well washed and dried, tough stems discarded

4 swordfish steaks, ³/₄ to 1 inch thick and 6 to 7 ounces each

Freshly ground black pepper

Sea salt

PREPARE THE TOMATOES   Halve the plum tomatoes and squeeze them over a small bowl to remove the seeds and collect any juices; dice the tomatoes. In a medium sauté pan, heat 1½ tablespoons of the olive oil over medium-high heat. Add the plum and cherry tomatoes and the collected tomato juices to the pan. Season with a couple pinches of salt and cook, stirring occasionally, until the cherry tomatoes release much of their juice. Add the olives, oregano, basil, and vinegar. Cook for a minute, stirring, then take the pan off the heat.

WILT THE WATERCRESS   In a small sauté pan, heat 1½ teaspoons of the olive oil over medium heat. Add the watercress and cook just until wilted. Take the pan off the heat.

GRILL THE SWORDFISH   Heat the grill of your choice or a grill pan to medium hot. Brush the swordfish with olive oil and season well with salt and pepper. Cook 3 to 4 minutes on each side. While the fish cooks, reheat the watercress and the tomato mixture, if necessary.

TO SERVE   Divide the tomato and olive mixture among four plates. Top with the swordfish and then place the watercress on top of the fish. Sprinkle a tiny bit of sea salt over the watercress.

CRISPY SKATE WITH PAN-ROASTED POTATOES, CAPER SALMORIGLIO, AND ZUCCHINI PUREE   SERVES 4

I love skate. Actually the wings of a ray, the boneless white fillets are firm and slightly sweet (similar to a scallop but not as cloying). The texture, though, is what can't be beat: tiny ridges that cook up wonderfully crisp and hold a sauce beautifully. Do ask your fishmonger to stock it. In a pinch, you can substitute halibut.

PAN-ROAST THE POTATOES   Heat 3 tablespoons of the olive oil in a medium sauté pan over medium heat. Add the potatoes and cook until tender and golden brown, increasing the heat, if necessary, and stirring occasionally, about 8 minutes. Keep warm.

SAUTÉ THE SKATE   Season the skate well with salt and pepper. Heat the remaining 2 tablespoons of olive oil in a large sauté pan over medium-high heat. Sauté the fish on one side until lightly browned, about 3 minutes. Turn and cook the other side until crispy and browned, another 1 to 2 minutes. (If you're using halibut, add a few minutes to the cooking time.)

TO SERVE   Spoon ⅓ to ½ cup of the Zucchini Puree in the center of four rimmed plates. Place the potatoes off to one side. Position a piece of fish in the center of the plate, partially covering the potatoes. Drizzle 1 to 2 tablespoons of the Caper Salmoriglio over and around the fish. Top the fish with a few greens, if you like, and finish each plate with a tiny sprinkle of sea salt.

5 tablespoons extra virgin olive oil

2 Yukon gold potatoes, cut into ½-inch dice

4 boneless, skinless skate fillets, 6 to 7 ounces each

Kosher salt and freshly ground black pepper

Zucchini Puree (recipe follows)

Caper Salmoriglio (recipe follows)

1 handful baby greens tossed with a little olive oil (optional)

Sea salt

ZUCCHINI PUREE

MAKES ABOUT 2 CUPS

This puree should be just thick enough that it will plop off a spoon and hold its shape briefly before settling. Delicious with the skate, it would also make a fine soup with the addition of some diced blanched vegetables (peas, carrots, leeks, zucchini) and a little more liquid. It would also go well as is with grilled chicken.

1 medium zucchini (14 to 15 ounces), ends trimmed

$1^1/_2$ tablespoons olive oil

Pinch of crushed red pepper flakes

$^1/_4$ teaspoon capers, preferably salt-packed, well rinsed

1 cup Chicken Broth (page 241)

Halve the zucchini lengthwise and scrape out any large seeds with a spoon. Chop the zucchini into ½-inch pieces. In a small saucepan, heat the olive oil over medium heat. Add the red pepper flakes and cook for 1 minute. Add the zucchini and cook, stirring occasionally, until just tender, about 7 minutes. Add the capers and the chicken broth and bring to a gentle boil. Puree well with a blender. The puree can be made a day ahead and kept refrigerated. Reheat it gently before serving.

CAPER SALMORIGLIO

MAKES ABOUT $^1/_2$ CUP

Off the Amalfi coast, they make a lemon, olive oil, and parsley sauce called salmoriglio to serve over fish. I like the punchier flavor of capers, especially with the juicy, full-flavored skate in the preceding recipe, so I make my version with capers and shallots. This sauce will keep for a couple of weeks refrigerated, so you may want to consider doubling it. It's delicious on all kinds of fish as well as drizzled over steamed potatoes and green beans for a very flavorful side dish.

$^1/_2$ cup extra virgin olive oil

2 tablespoons capers, preferably salt-packed, well rinsed

1 small fresh thyme sprig

Pinch of crushed red pepper flakes, or more to taste

2 small shallots, thinly sliced

In a small saucepan, combine the olive oil, capers, thyme, red pepper flakes, and shallots. Heat over medium-low heat for 20 minutes. If making ahead, gently reheat before serving.

BLACK COD WITH CARAMELIZED FENNEL AND CONCENTRATED TOMATOES SERVES 4

What I love about this dish is that despite the intensity of the accompaniments—fennel that's roasted until it's sweet and tender and tomatoes cooked to a deeper flavor—you still can taste the fish. (In the Italian Marches, this method of cooking is called *in porchetta* as these flavors are more traditionally paired with pork.) The Concentrated Tomatoes called for in this dish are easy to make, but they do need some unattended time in the oven, so plan accordingly.

12 whole baby fennel bulbs, trimmed, or 2 regular-size bulbs, trimmed and cut into sixths

Kosher salt

6 tablespoons extra virgin olive oil

6 to 8 whole fingerling potatoes (about 10 ounces)

8 halves Concentrated Tomatoes (recipe follows)

4 skinless black cod fillets, 6 to 8 ounces each

Freshly ground black pepper

1 small fresh rosemary sprig

2 tablespoons chopped fresh parsley

Sea salt

PREPARE THE VEGETABLES   Heat the oven to 350°F. Put the fennel in a small ovenproof pan and season lightly with salt. Add 3 tablespoons of the olive oil and 1 tablespoon water to the pan, cover with a lid or aluminum foil, and roast until just tender, about 30 minutes. Remove the cover and roast for another 20 minutes to brown the fennel well. (The fennel can be roasted ahead of time and kept at room temperature for a couple of hours.)

About 20 minutes before serving, put the potatoes in a small saucepan and cover with well-salted water. Bring to a boil and cook until tender, about 10 minutes. Drain, cool briefly, and slice lengthwise about ⅓ inch thick.

Heat a sauté pan over medium-low heat and lightly coat the bottom of the pan with olive oil. Add the tomato halves, the fennel, and the potatoes and heat through.

SEAR THE FISH   Heat a large sauté pan over medium heat. Put 2 tablespoons of olive oil in the pan. Season the fish with salt and pepper and, when the oil is very hot, add it to the pan with its better-looking side down. Cook until golden brown, 2 to 3 minutes. Flip the fish over and add the rosemary to the pan to infuse the oil with its flavor. Cook for 1 or 2 minutes longer on the second side, until the fish is golden brown and pulls away easily from the pan.

TO SERVE   Divide the vegetables among four warm plates, piling them in the middle. Place a fillet on top with its better side facing up. If there is any oil left in the pan, drizzle it over the fish. Sprinkle with the parsley and a little sea salt and serve immediately.

CONCENTRATED TOMATOES
MAKES ABOUT 30 HALVES

These tomatoes are one of my pantry staples, which is why this recipe makes more than needed for the preceding black cod recipe. Try them alongside grilled chicken or sautéed shrimp, in bean dishes, on panini, or chopped and tossed with some pasta and fresh basil. They'll keep almost a week in the fridge and you can even freeze them, which affects their texture only slightly.

3 pounds plum tomatoes, halved and gently seeded

$1/4$ cup extra virgin olive oil, plus more if needed

1 teaspoon chopped fresh oregano

$1^1/2$ teaspoons chopped fresh rosemary

1 teaspoon sugar

Kosher salt and freshly ground black pepper

Heat the oven to 300°F. Toss the tomatoes with enough olive oil to coat them liberally (about ¼ cup) and lay them cut side down on a sided baking sheet. Sprinkle the oregano, rosemary, and sugar over them and season lightly with salt and pepper.

Cook the tomatoes until they are quite concentrated with a very deep red color; this will take 3½ to 4 hours. They should look quite dry on the outside but retain some moisture within. Cool to room temperature, peel away the loose skins, and store in an airtight container in the refrigerator.

SEARED BASS WITH ASPARAGUS PUREE AND ASPARAGUS POTATO CAKES SERVES 6

I like to cook Mediterranean sea bass (called *branzino* in Italian and *loup de mer* in French) because it's sweeter and creamier than wild striped bass and black bass, both of which cook similarly. This seared fish is so simple that I like to give it an accompaniment that's a little special, which these Asparagus Potato Cakes, especially if made with the preserved truffles, definitely are. (To tip the scale even further, you can add some lump crabmeat to the mix as well.) Though this dish requires more pans than some, it's all pretty straightforward cooking. Plus, not everything has to be done at the last minute. You can make the puree a day or so ahead and the potato cakes can sit in a warm oven while you sear the fish.

MAKE THE ASPARAGUS PUREE   Peel the asparagus if very fibrous and chop it into ½-inch pieces. Heat 1 tablespoon of the olive oil in a small saucepan over medium-high heat. Add the shallot, the red pepper flakes, and a large pinch of salt. Cook, stirring occasionally, until the shallot is tender and taking on some color, about 5 minutes. Add the asparagus and cook for about 1 minute. Add the broth plus ¼ cup of water and bring to a boil. Reduce the heat to a robust simmer and cook until the asparagus is tender, about 5 minutes. Let cool a bit, then puree with a blender, adding 1½ teaspoons more olive oil. Transfer the puree to a clean small saucepan and reserve. (The puree can be made ahead and refrigerated for a day.)

SEAR THE FISH   Season the bass with salt and pepper. Heat 2 to 3 tablespoons of olive oil in a very large sauté pan over medium-high heat. When very hot, add the fish, flesh side down, and cook until nicely browned, about 3 minutes. Flip the fish over and continue cooking, skin side down, for another 2 or 3 minutes, depending on the thickness of the fillet. Be careful not to overcook it, as it will continue to cook off the heat. I usually take it off the heat when I can feel a slight separation of the flesh. If you want to take a peek, look for the flesh to be almost opaque but not quite flaking.

(continued)

½ bunch asparagus (about ½ pound), tough ends trimmed

4 to 5 tablespoons extra virgin olive oil

1 medium shallot, sliced lengthwise into thin slivers

Pinch of crushed red pepper flakes

Kosher salt and freshly ground black pepper

1 cup Chicken Broth (page 241)

6 sea bass, striped bass, or black bass fillets, about 6 ounces each, scaled and boned but preferably with skin

Asparagus Potato Cakes (recipe follows)

TO SERVE   Reheat the asparagus puree if necessary. Spoon a few tablespoons of the puree on one side of each plate. Position a potato cake near and slightly overlapping the puree. Angle a fillet against the cake. Garnish the plate with blanched asparagus tips, if you like, and serve immediately.

ASPARAGUS POTATO CAKES

SERVES 6

Once you get the gist of how these cakes are made, you can play with the formula, subbing, say, peas and chives for the asparagus and shallot. For an even more refined presentation, cook the cakes in bottomless four-inch ring molds right in the sauté pan. These cakes are delicious with a roast chicken, too.

3 medium Yukon gold or new potatoes (about
    $1^1/_4$ pounds), peeled and quartered

1 teaspoon kosher salt, plus more for cooking

$^1/_2$ bunch asparagus (about $^1/_2$ pound), tough ends trimmed

$^1/_4$ cup extra virgin olive oil, plus more if needed

1 large shallot, sliced lengthwise into thin slivers
    (about $^1/_3$ cup)

Pinch of crushed red pepper flakes

2 tablespoons finely chopped preserved truffle
    (optional)

1 whole egg

2 egg yolks

Freshly ground black pepper

$^1/_3$ to $^1/_2$ cup all-purpose flour, plus more for flouring
    your hands

MASH THE POTATOES   Place the potatoes in a small saucepan, cover with salted water by 2 inches, and bring to a boil. Boil until just tender, about 15 minutes, and drain. Mash the potatoes but not until perfectly smooth. Transfer to a medium bowl and let cool so they're not piping hot when you add the rest of the ingredients.

PREPARE THE ASPARAGUS   Remove the tips from the asparagus and reserve for another use or blanch them for an optional garnish. Diagonally slice the stems ⅛ inch thick. In a small sauté pan, heat about 1 tablespoon of the olive oil over medium-high heat and cook the shallot until lightly browned on the edges, 3 to 5 minutes. Add the red pepper flakes, cook for a minute, then add the asparagus. Sauté until just crisp-tender, 3 to 5 minutes.

Add the asparagus to the potatoes along with the truffle, if using, the whole egg, and the yolks. Season well with 1 teaspoon salt and a few grinds of pepper. Stir in ⅓ cup of the flour, adding more, up to about ½ cup total, until the mixture is moist but not wet.

TO FINISH   Heat the oven to 200°F. Have ready a small baking sheet. Heat the remaining 3 tablespoons olive oil in a large sauté pan over high heat. With lightly floured hands, scoop up about one sixth of the batter and pat it into a pancake ¾ inch thick. After shaping each cake, slip it into the hot oil and then flatten it gently with the back of a spatula. (Depending on the size of your pan, you may have to cook the cakes in batches.) Fry the cakes until well browned on one side, 2 to 3 minutes, adjusting the heat as needed. Turn the cakes over and brown the other side well. (Alternatively, you can shape all of the cakes ahead, set them on a lightly floured plate, and chill for up to an hour; they may stick a little as you transfer them from the plate, but you can reshape them with the spatula once in the pan.)

Transfer the potato cakes to the baking sheet and finish cooking in the warm oven for at least 5 minutes, and up to 15 minutes, before serving.

SLOW-ROASTED SALMON WITH TRUMPET MUSHROOMS AND TURNIPS SERVES 4

I cook most fish on the stove over pretty high heat, but I treat salmon more like I do beefsteak, searing it well and then finishing it in a low oven to a wonderful medium rare.

4 salmon fillets, about 6 ounces each, with skin

Kosher salt and freshly ground black pepper

3 to 4 tablespoons extra virgin olive oil

14 baby turnips or 2 or 3 small turnips (about 1 pound), cut into $^1/_2$-inch pieces and blanched

4 scallions, white and light green parts, cut into 1-inch lengths

$^1/_2$ cup diced potatoes, blanched

1 cup coarsely chopped mushrooms, preferably trumpet mushrooms

Pinch of crushed red pepper flakes

1 cup Chicken Broth (page 241)

Chopped fresh chives (optional)

SLOW-ROAST THE SALMON   Heat the oven to 250°F. Season the salmon on both sides with salt and pepper. Heat 1 to 2 tablespoons of the olive oil in a large ovenproof sauté pan over medium-high heat. Add the salmon, skin side down, and cook until the skin is browned and crisp, about 5 minutes. Transfer the pan to the oven and let the salmon slowly finish cooking to medium rare, about 15 minutes.

SIMMER THE VEGETABLES   Meanwhile, in a medium sauté pan, heat 2 tablespoons of the olive oil over medium-high heat. Add the turnips and scallions, season with a pinch of salt, and cook, stirring occasionally, until the turnips are lightly browned. Add the potatoes, mushrooms, and red pepper flakes and sauté for another minute or two. Add the chicken broth and simmer the vegetables gently until tender while the salmon finishes cooking.

TO SERVE   Divide the vegetables among four warm plates and top with the salmon, skin side up. Finish with a sprinkling of chives, if you like.

ROASTED ORATA WITH SUMMER SQUASH AND CIPOLLINI AGRODOLCE SERVES 4

If you can't find orata, a sea bream that also goes by the names *dorade* and *dorado,* use its more commonly found cousin—snapper. Both deliver the rich, succulent, meaty flavor this sweet and sour dish needs.

PREPARE THE VEGETABLES   In a medium sauté pan, heat 1 to 2 teaspoons of the olive oil over medium-high heat, add the carrot, and cook until tender and just lightly colored, about 4 minutes. Remove the carrot and reserve. In the same pan, heat 1 tablespoon of the olive oil over medium-high heat, add the leek and thyme, season with a little salt, and cook, stirring occasionally, until the leek is lightly colored and begins to soften. Add a few tablespoons of the broth if needed to keep the leeks from browning too much. Add another tablespoon of olive oil and the zucchini and pattypans. Cook, stirring, until the squash is lightly browned, about 5 minutes, again adding broth as needed to keep the vegetables from sticking and overbrowning. The broth should help them steam. Add the parsley and chives and remove from the heat.

SAUTÉ THE FISH   In a separate sauté pan, heat 1 to 2 tablespoons of the olive oil over high heat. Season the fish well with salt and place skin side down in the hot pan. Cook until nicely browned, 3 to 4 minutes. Flip the fish over, cook another minute, then remove from the heat and let the residual heat from the pan finish cooking the fish.

TO SERVE   Reheat the vegetables briefly, if need be, and divide them among four warm plates. Place the fish on top of the vegetables. Spoon some of the Cipollini Agrodolce around the fish and vegetables and serve immediately.

(continued)

- 4 to 5 tablespoons extra virgin olive oil
- 1 medium carrot, finely diced
- 1 small leek, trimmed, diced, and rinsed
- 1 thyme sprig
- Kosher salt
- $1/4$ to $1/3$ cup Chicken Broth (page 241)
- 8 ounces baby zucchini (about 12), trimmed and sliced $1/8$ inch thick
- 8 ounces baby pattypan squash (about 16), trimmed and sliced $1/8$ inch thick
- 1 teaspoon finely chopped fresh parsley
- 1 teaspoon finely chopped fresh chives
- 4 orata fillets, 5 to 6 ounces each, with skin
- Cipollini Agrodolce (recipe follows)

CIPOLLINI AGRODOLCE

MAKES ABOUT 2 CUPS

These flavorful onions would make a delicious garnish with other main courses; fragrant roast chicken comes to mind, as does grilled lamb. The onions will keep for four or five days, refrigerated.

1 tablespoon extra virgin olive oil

$^3/_4$ pound cipollini onions, cut in half if large

Kosher salt

1 tablespoon sugar

2 tablespoons red wine vinegar, or more to taste

1$^1/_2$ cups Chicken Broth (page 241), plus more if needed

2 small fresh thyme sprigs

Pinch of crushed red pepper flakes

Heat a sauté pan over medium-high heat. Add the olive oil and when hot, add the onions. Season lightly with salt and cook, stirring occasionally, until lightly browned, about 5 minutes. Add the sugar and let it caramelize for a few minutes, further browning the onions. Add the vinegar and shake the pan to coat the onions well. Add the broth, thyme, and red pepper flakes. Cover and cook until the onions are quite tender, another 12 to 15 minutes, depending on their size; the sauce should still have a good amount of liquid. Taste and add more vinegar if you like.

TURBOT WITH CARAMELIZED ENDIVE, LENTILS, AND SALSA VERDE SERVES 4

I love this dish because it hits all sides of the palate: The bitter endive is sweetened by long cooking while the Salsa Verde adds salt and tang as well as color. You can substitute halibut for the turbot, but turbot is worth seeking out, especially if it comes from European waters. This is a dish I could eat every day.

COOK THE VEGETABLES   Heat the oven to 300°F. Cut the endives and leeks into ⅜-inch rounds and wash the leeks well. Heat 2 tablespoons of the olive oil in a large sauté pan over medium heat. Add the endives, leeks, and sliced onions and season with a little salt. Cook, stirring occasionally, until golden brown; the vegetables don't have to be tender at this point. Transfer the vegetables to a baking dish and bake, tossing occasionally, until completely cooked and soft, about 35 minutes.

COOK THE LENTILS   In a medium saucepan, heat 2 tablespoons of the olive oil over medium heat. Add the diced onion, carrot, and celery and cook until tender, about 5 minutes. Add the thyme, lentils, and enough broth to cover by 1 inch. Reduce the heat and simmer, adding more broth if necessary, until tender, 20 to 25 minutes.

SAUTÉ THE FISH   In a large sauté pan, heat the remaining 2 tablespoons of olive oil over high heat. Season the turbot well with salt and place skin side down in the hot pan. Cook until nicely browned, 3 to 4 minutes. Flip the fish over, cook another minute, then remove from heat and let the residual heat from the pan finish cooking the fish.

TO SERVE   Divide the lentils among four serving plates, positioning them in the center of the plate. Top the lentils with the vegetables and then the fish. Dribble the Salsa Verde around and over the fish and serve.

2 Belgian endives

3 medium leeks, trimmed, white and light green parts only

6 tablespoons extra virgin olive oil

3 small onions, 2 thinly sliced and 1 finely diced

Kosher salt

1/2 medium carrot, finely diced

1 celery stalk, finely diced

2 small fresh thyme sprigs

1 cup lentils

3 cups Chicken Broth (page 241)

4 turbot fillets, about 6 ounces each, with skin

Salsa Verde (recipe follows)

SALSA VERDE

MAKES ABOUT 2 CUPS

Similar to a South American chimichurri sauce, this is a wonderful condiment to have on hand, which is why this makes more than you need for the turbot recipe it's paired with. (It will keep for a week refrigerated, but serve it warm.) Try it with grilled lamb or skirt steak.

1 to 1^1/$_2$ cups extra virgin olive oil

^{1}/$_2$ bunch parsley, including tender stems, well washed and coarsely chopped

^{1}/$_2$ cup drained, jarred cocktail onions

3 anchovy fillets, preferably salt-packed, well rinsed

1 tablespoon capers, preferably salt-packed, well rinsed

^{1}/$_2$ cup pitted green olives

^{1}/$_4$ cup drained cornichons

Combine 1 cup of the olive oil and the parsley in a food processor or blender and puree. Add the onions, anchovies, capers, olives, and cornichons and puree until smooth and slightly chunky, adding more olive oil as necessary to achieve that consistency.

STEWED OCTOPUS WITH SHERRY VINEGAR SERVES 3 TO 4

If you've never had octopus, it may be hard to believe that these odd-looking, suction cup–studded tentacles can cook up so tender. The trick, as with squid (which you can substitute for the octopus), is to cook it either very quickly over high heat or long and low, as I do here; during cooking the octopus reduces in size. The sherry vinegar may seem a bit harsh when first added, but it mellows over the course of the cooking. This spicy, oceany, rustic stew would be perfect to eat in front of a fire in fall.

4 fresh or frozen octopus, about 1 pound each, cleaned

3 to 4 tablespoons extra virgin olive oil

1 large shallot, thinly sliced lengthwise (about $1/3$ cup)

Pinch of crushed red pepper flakes

Kosher salt

1 to 1 $1/2$ cups Chicken Broth (page 241)

3 tablespoons sherry vinegar

2 tablespoons crushed tomatoes

3 to 4 medium fingerling potatoes (about 5 ounces), diced

1 cup cherry tomatoes, quartered

8 scallions, light green part, finely sliced on the diagonal

$1/2$ teaspoon fresh thyme leaves

STEW THE OCTOPUS   Cut the tentacles off the octopus heads. If you would like to use the heads in the stew, turn them inside out, remove the beaks and ink sacs with a paring knife, and slice the heads thinly.

Heat the oven to 350°F. In a high-sided ovenproof sauté pan, heat 1 tablespoon of the olive oil over medium heat. Add the shallot and red pepper flakes. Season with a pinch of salt and cook, stirring occasionally, until the shallot is golden, about 5 minutes. Increase the heat to medium-high and add the octopus. Cook, stirring, until the tentacles begin to curl. Add enough broth to come about halfway up the sides of the tentacles. (As they cook, the tentacles will shrink considerably while releasing a lot of liquid.) Add the vinegar and the crushed tomatoes and stir to combine. Cover the pan and cook in the oven until the octopus is very tender, 45 to 50 minutes.

This is one of my favorite dishes.

COOK THE VEGETABLES   Heat 1 to 2 tablespoons of the olive oil in a large sauté pan over medium heat. Cook the potatoes until lightly browned and no longer hard, about 6 minutes. Add the cherry tomatoes, all but a teaspoon of the scallions, and the thyme, and cook another minute. Remove from the heat until the octopus is ready.

TO SERVE   When the octopus is tender, pour its cooking liquid into the pan of vegetables. Bring to a simmer and cook until the potatoes are just tender, 3 to 4 minutes. Divide the vegetables and sauce among warm bowls. Top with the octopus, a sprinkling of the remaining scallion, and a drizzle of olive oil, and serve.

MOIST-ROASTED WHOLE RED SNAPPER WITH TOMATOES, BASIL, AND OREGANO SERVES 3 to 4

I have to say, I am very glad we included a photograph of this dish, because words alone can't convey how magnificent, how beautifully ceremonial, a whole fish looks when presented at the table. I'm always excited when a few friends and I settle in to devour one. (And devour we do; you should see what little is left when we're through with it.) Aside from being so good-looking, a whole fish also offers much more flavor than fillets because the head and the bones add depth to the accompanying sauce. A completely gratifying dish.

One 2^1/2- to 3-pound whole (head on) red snapper, scaled and cleaned

Kosher salt and freshly ground black pepper

1 lemon, half sliced and half left whole

10 fresh basil leaves, plus 1 tablespoon chopped

5 small fresh oregano sprigs, plus 1^1/2 teaspoons chopped

4 to 5 tablespoons extra virgin olive oil

^{1}/4 teaspoon crushed red pepper flakes

1^1/2 cups cherry tomatoes (about 8 ounces), cut in half

6 to 8 fingerling potatoes (about 10 ounces), cut into ^{3}/4-inch dice and blanched

1 cup Chicken Broth (page 241)

STUFF AND COOK THE SNAPPER   Heat the oven to 325°F. If the fins are still on the fish, use kitchen scissors to cut them off (they just fall apart when cooked). Season both the inside and the outside of the fish liberally with salt and pepper. Stuff the cavity with the lemon slices, whole basil leaves, and oregano sprigs.

Using a very large (14-inch) ovenproof sauté pan or a small roasting pan, heat about 2 tablespoons of the olive oil over medium-high heat until smoking. Add the fish and cook until well browned on one side, about 3 minutes. Flip the fish over—use a large spatula and grab the tail if it's not too hot—and brown the other side, about 2 minutes. Remove the fish and use wadded paper towels to wipe the oil from the pan.

Add another tablespoon of olive oil to the pan plus the red pepper flakes, tomatoes, and potatoes and cook until the tomatoes begin to release their liquid, about 3 minutes.

Return the fish to the pan, laying it on top of the vegetables, and drizzle about a tablespoon of olive oil over it. Add the chicken broth and squeeze the remaining lemon half into the sauce. Cook on the stove another few minutes, basting the fish with the sauce and moving some of the tomatoes and potatoes on top of the fish.

Finish cooking the fish in the oven, 18 to 20 minutes. (To check for doneness, push the head down gently in the area between the nose and the top of the head; when the head easily moves away from the back of the neck, it is ready.)

TO SERVE   Remove the fish from the oven and carefully transfer it to a sided platter, pouring any liquid in its cavity back into the pan; keep the fish warm. Return the pan to the stove over medium heat and cook the sauce and vegetables for a minute or two to concentrate the flavors. Add another tablespoon of olive oil, the chopped basil and oregano, and additional salt and pepper if necessary. Pour the sauce and vegetables over the fish and serve, using a large spoon to remove portions of fish. (Don't forget to turn it over to eat the other side!)

MOIST-ROASTED WHOLE RED SNAPPER WITH TOMATOES, BASIL, AND OREGANO, page 148

SPRINGTIME SOFT-SHELL CRAB WITH PEA PUREE SERVES 4

Imagine taking a walk on a beach on a warm spring day. That's what this dish reminds me of. You have these bright, slightly crisp vegetables, which get transformed by the juices from the crab, joining them with the flavors of the sea. Tarragon and parsley add a welcome note from the herb garden, while a hint of smoky bacon reminds you that it's not quite summer. Like lobster, soft-shell crab is best when purchased alive. You can have the crabs cleaned by the fishmonger, but cook them on the same day you buy them. Even better, bring them home alive and clean them yourself as directed in the note. To get the best flavor from the crab—it really is quite amazing when mixed with the pea puree—be sure not to overcook it.

MAKE A PEA PUREE   In a small saucepan, heat 1 tablespoon of the olive oil over medium heat. Add the shallot, season with a generous pinch of salt, and cook until tender, about 5 minutes. Add half of the peas and 1 cup chicken broth. Increase the heat to medium-high and cook the peas until tender, 2 to 3 minutes. Add the tarragon and parsley. Transfer the mixture to a blender or food processor (or use a hand blender right in the pot) and puree it. (You can make the pea puree ahead and refrigerate it; rewarm it before serving and thin it with a little broth if necessary.)

CRISP THE BACON   In a sauté pan, cook the bacon until crispy, adding a teaspoon or so of olive oil, if needed. Remove from the pan, reserve in a warm place, and wipe the pan clean.

COOK THE VEGETABLES   In the same pan, heat ½ to 1 tablespoon of the olive oil over medium heat. Add the remaining peas, the asparagus, green beans, carrot, and scallions. Season with a little salt and cook, stirring occasionally to keep the vegetables from browning, until the vegetables are crisp-tender. (Add a little water if needed to prevent browning.) Divide the vegetables and then the pea puree among four wide bowls or rimmed plates; keep the bowls warm while you fry the crabs.

(continued)

2 tablespoons extra virgin olive oil

1 shallot, thinly sliced lengthwise

1 tablespoon kosher salt, plus more for seasoning

1 cup frozen peas

1 to 1¼ cups Chicken Broth (page 241)

1 tablespoon chopped fresh tarragon, plus more for garnish

1 teaspoon chopped fresh parsley, plus more for garnish

2 slices bacon, preferably thick cut, sliced crosswise into ¼-inch-thick lardons

1 cup very thinly sliced asparagus (about 10 stalks)

1 cup very thinly sliced green beans

½ cup finely diced carrot

½ cup thinly sliced scallions

1 cup all-purpose flour

1 tablespoon paprika

Freshly ground black pepper

About 2 cups soy or peanut oil for frying

4 soft-shell crabs, cleaned

FRY THE CRABS On a plate, combine the flour with the tablespoon of salt, the paprika, and a few grinds of pepper. Position the flour mixture near the stove. Also have a few layers of paper towels nearby for draining the crabs.

In a sauté pan large enough to hold the 4 crabs with a little space around them, pour soy or peanut oil to come about ⅓ inch up the sides of the pan. Heat over medium-high heat until the oil is quite hot. Dredge a crab in the flour mixture, coating both sides well. Shake off the excess flour and place the crab in the hot oil "shell" side down. Let the crabs get golden brown on one side and then flip. (Be careful while the crabs are frying; sometimes they pop and spray their now hot juices. If they're spraying a lot, use a paring knife to poke a hole or two in the belly.) Cook for another 3 to 4 minutes on the second side. Remove them from the oil and drain briefly on paper towels.

TO SERVE Place a crab in each bowl. (A fun way to present them is to cut the crabs in half, placing one half down in the bowl and the other half standing up with its legs facing up and out of the bowl.) Divide the bacon among the bowls, garnish with a little tarragon and parsley, and serve immediately.

NOTE To clean live crabs: Cut off the head approximately ¼ inch below the eyes. Press on the crab a little to squeeze out a green bubble. Remove the gill filaments on each side of the crab by peeling back the pointed soft shell and scraping these inedible gills out with a paring knife. On the belly side, bend back the apron (or tail flap) and pull using a slight twisting motion. Refrigerate until ready to use.

ROASTED LOBSTER WITH PEPERONATA SERVES 2

Parcooking lobsters whole in their shells (as opposed to cut into pieces, as some chefs cook them) prevents the lobster meat from becoming waterlogged. You can also serve this as an appetizer for four, with half a lobster per person.

PARCOOK THE LOBSTERS   Bring to a boil a pot of salted water large enough to hold the lobsters. Put the lobsters in head first, cover if you like, and cook for 3 minutes. (You're cooking just enough to make removing the meat easy; the lobster will finish cooking in the oven.) Remove the lobsters from the pot. When cool enough to handle, remove the meat from the large claws and the tails. Cut the tails lengthwise and remove the intestinal tract. Arrange the pieces on a baking sheet with the tails' cut side up. Cover and refrigerate until ready to roast. (You can parcook the lobsters a day in advance.)

MAKE THE TOPPING   In a small bowl, toss together the bread crumbs, parsley, olive oil, lemon juice, and chives. Season with a couple pinches of salt and a few grinds of pepper.

FINISH COOKING THE LOBSTER   Heat the oven to 250°F. Spread the bread crumb mixture over the lobster meat and cook until the lobster is just cooked through, 8 to 10 minutes. Brown the bread crumbs, if you like, by briefly setting the pan under the broiler.

TO SERVE   Divide the peperonata between two plates and lay the lobster pieces on top. Serve immediately.   *(continued)*

Kosher salt

2 lobsters, about 1^1/2 pounds each

^{1}/2 cup fresh bread crumbs

1^1/2 teaspoons chopped fresh parsley

^{1}/4 cup extra virgin olive oil

^{1}/4 cup fresh lemon juice

1^1/2 teaspoons finely chopped fresh chives

Freshly ground black pepper

Peperonata (recipe follows)

PEPERONATA

SERVES 2

Peperonata can also be served on its own as an antipasto and makes a colorful accompaniment to roast chicken.

$^1/_4$ cup extra virgin olive oil

1 medium onion, cut into a large dice (about 1 cup)

2 garlic cloves, very thinly sliced

$^1/_4$ teaspoon crushed red pepper flakes, or more to taste

Kosher salt

1 red bell pepper, stemmed, seeded, and cut into a large dice (about 1 cup)

2 plum tomatoes, seeded and cut into a large dice (about 1 cup)

Up to $^1/_4$ cup Chicken Broth (page 241), if necessary

1 tablespoon chopped fresh basil

1 tablespoon chopped fresh parsley

Heat the oven to 350°F. Heat the olive oil in an ovenproof sauté pan over medium-low heat. Add the onion, garlic, and red pepper flakes. Season with a pinch of salt and cook, stirring occasionally, until the onion begins to turn light brown, about 20 minutes. Add the bell pepper and tomatoes and cook, stirring occasionally, until the tomatoes begin to release their liquid, about 10 minutes. Cover the pan with a lid or foil and bake until the peppers are very tender, about 20 minutes. If the oil has begun to separate from the mixture, stir in a little chicken broth. Toss the peperonata with the basil and parsley and serve hot or at room temperature.

POULTRY

Even though some of us pretend otherwise, we all love chicken. Maybe it's because it was the favorite of our childhood (did *anybody* like lamb as a kid?), maybe it's because its flavor is so consistent and goes with just about anything, or maybe it's that perfectly crisped chicken skin is flat-out, undeniably delicious. Whatever the reasons, chicken is what most people cook most often at home. Conversely, chicken gets barely a nod on the menus of most fine restaurants. With that dichotomy in mind, the recipes here are more in line with rustic, soul-satisfying, home-cooked fare—including a one-pan chicken dish inspired by one my mom used to make—than restaurant plates. But my intention is not to bore; I do a whole roast chicken featuring classic flavors like rosemary and thyme, but adding an ample amount of fresh ginger takes it in a whole new aromatic direction without interfering with the raison d'être of roast chicken, which is pure comfort.

I've included a recipe for rabbit in this chapter because chicken thighs could substitute for the tender meat found on rabbit legs. But do give rabbit a try. More and more supermarkets carry rabbit these days, and it, as well as quail (featured on page 172), is a welcome change from ubiquitous, albeit well-loved, chicken.

PAN-ROASTED CHICKEN WITH POTATOES AND GREEN OLIVES SERVES 4

My mother used to make something like this when I was a kid, and I loved it. I've tried a few times to get the chicken to taste just like hers, but memory is a funny thing; I've never felt I've gotten it quite right, and she doesn't remember what recipe I'm talking about. This may not be exactly what my mom made, but it's simple, fairly quick, and quite satisfying nonetheless. I like to use large, meaty green olives to finish the dish. As for the chicken, my preference is for dark meat only; if you do add bone-in chicken breast, cut it in half with a cleaver to better fit in the pan. Whatever you do, don't think too hard about this dish; it's dinner, not dining.

BROWN THE CHICKEN   In a wide, heavy-based sauté or frying pan, preferably cast iron, heat the oil over medium-high heat. Season the chicken well with salt and a lot of black pepper. Add the chicken, skin side down, and cook until the skin is well browned and crisp, about 10 minutes. Turn the chicken, reduce the heat to medium, partially cover the pan (another pan, inverted, can take the place of a lid), and continue cooking another 15 minutes.

TO FINISH   Add the onion to the pan. Continue cooking, stirring the onion occasionally, for about 10 minutes. Add the potatoes and continue cooking, stirring occasionally, until the potatoes are tender and the chicken is cooked through—the juices from a thigh will run clear when pricked with a fork—another 10 to 15 minutes. Add the olives and cook for a few more minutes just to warm them through. Serve immediately.

2 tablespoons extra virgin olive oil

One 3- to 3^1/2-pound chicken, cut into 8 pieces, or 3 pounds legs and thighs

Kosher salt and freshly ground black pepper

1 medium onion, chopped (about 1 cup)

8 to 10 fingerling or 2 to 3 Yukon gold potatoes, cut into 1^1/2-inch pieces (about 1^1/2 cups)

^{1}/2 cup coarsely chopped pitted green olives

WHOLE ROAST CHICKEN WITH PUMPKIN, MUSHROOMS, AND GINGER SERVES 3 TO 4

Though ginger may seem unusual in an Italian kitchen, I really like how it adds an unexpected but welcome warm flavor to the Italian aromatics I turn to again and again. It also perfectly complements the pumpkin for an autumnal dish. As an added bonus for using it, I get to put the word *zenzero* (Italian for ginger) on my menu. Great word, isn't it?

4 tablespoons ($^1/_2$ stick) unsalted butter

2 tablespoons extra virgin olive oil

One 4-inch piece fresh ginger, peeled

6 small fresh thyme sprigs

4 small fresh rosemary sprigs

4 garlic cloves, crushed

One 3$^1/_2$- to 4-pound chicken, excess fat and skin trimmed, patted dry

1 teaspoon kosher salt

2 cups shiitake mushroom caps

1 large onion, cut into 8 wedges

1 small sugar pumpkin, cut into 8 wedges, seeds removed

Heat the oven to 375°F.

FLAVOR THE BUTTER   In a small saucepan, heat the butter and oil over low heat. Slice half of the ginger into thin rounds and reserve. Grate the rest of the ginger into the pan. Add the thyme, rosemary, and garlic. Bring to a simmer, reduce the heat to very low, and let the aromatics steep for 10 minutes.

ROAST THE CHICKEN AND VEGETABLES   Brush the flavored butter lavishly over the outside and inside of the chicken. Put the aromatics from the pan and the ginger rounds inside the bird's cavity. Season the chicken all over, inside and out, with about a teaspoon of salt. Put the chicken in a large roasting pan (you want enough room around the chicken to hold the vegetables in a single layer), and add the mushroom caps, onion, and pumpkin wedges (skin side down). Roast the chicken until done, periodically basting it with the fragrant juices that accumulate, 1 to 1 ½ hours depending on the size of the bird. (When cooked through, the juices from a pricked thigh will run clear and a thermometer inserted in the thigh will read 170°F.) Let the bird sit for 10 minutes before carving.

TO SERVE   Serve the chicken pieces with a mix of the roasted vegetables from the pan.

WHOLE ROAST CHICKEN *IN POTACCHIO* SERVES 3 TO 4

Cooking with onion, tomatoes, white wine, and rosemary—*in potacchio*—is typical of the Marches on the coast of Italy. Here, I present those flavors quite purely in an easy roast chicken. What I'm looking for when I make this dish is not so much a sauce, but a chunky, somewhat sticky, oily, flavor-packed accompaniment to the chicken. (I know those are not the most appetizing of words, but it's really good stuff.) Basting the chicken with the wine and tomato creates a true caramelization that should darken the skin beautifully; it also helps keep the chicken *morbido,* or moist. Adding potatoes and onions to the pan gives you an instant side dish, but you may still want to serve this with some good crusty bread or even some cooked pasta to soak up the lovely sauce.

ROAST THE CHICKEN AND VEGETABLES   Heat the oven to 375°F. Rub the chicken all over with 1 or 2 tablespoons of olive oil and season it well with salt inside and out. Put the chicken in a large roasting pan (you want enough room around the chicken to hold the vegetables in a single layer). Add the potatoes, rosemary, onion, tomatoes, and wine to the pan. Drizzle a tablespoon or so of olive oil and sprinkle a pinch of red pepper flakes over all.

Roast the chicken until done, periodically basting it with the liquid that accumulates, 1 to 1½ hours depending on the size of the bird. (When cooked through, the juices from a pricked thigh will run clear and a thermometer inserted in the thigh will read 170°F.) Let the bird sit for 10 minutes before carving.

TO SERVE   Serve the chicken pieces with the potatoes and onions. Spoon out some of the tomato "sauce" and add that to the plate, too.

One 3½- to 4-pound chicken, excess fat and skin trimmed, patted dry

2 to 3 tablespoons extra virgin olive oil

Kosher salt

6 medium new potatoes, quartered

6 small fresh rosemary sprigs

1 large onion, cut into 8 wedges

1 cup canned crushed tomatoes

1 cup dry white wine

Pinch of crushed red pepper flakes

BONELESS ROAST CHICKEN WITH ROASTED ROOT VEGETABLES SERVES 2 TO 3

This chicken is one of the few things I cook in a really hot oven. After browning the skin on the stove, I finish the chicken skin side down in the oven. As the juices release and evaporate, they essentially steam-roast the bird, resulting in very tender meat. And I love the luxuriousness of slicing into chicken that's been boned but not skinned; eating it this way feels very civilized and refined. If you don't want to bone a whole bird yourself, substitute a mix of boneless, skin-on breasts and thighs equaling 3 to $3^{1}/_{2}$ pounds.

One $3^{1}/_{2}$- to 4-pound chicken, split in half and boned

4 to 5 tablespoons extra virgin olive oil

Leaves from 2 small fresh rosemary sprigs

3 garlic cloves, sliced

Kosher salt and freshly ground black pepper

Roasted Root Vegetables (recipe follows)

MARINATE THE CHICKEN   In a baking dish or large zip-top bag, combine the chicken and 2 tablespoons of the olive oil, the rosemary, and the garlic. Let sit at room temperature for half an hour or refrigerate for up to 24 hours.

ROAST THE CHICKEN   Heat the oven to 500°F. Season the chicken well with salt and pepper. Heat 2 to 3 tablespoons of olive oil in an ovenproof sauté pan large enough to hold both halves of the bird. (Or divide the oil among two smaller pans.) Sear the chicken, skin side down, until very well browned, about 10 minutes. Pop the pan (or pans) into the hot oven to finish cooking, about 15 minutes. (When cooked through, the juices from a pricked thigh will run clear and a thermometer inserted in the thigh will read 170°F.)

TO SERVE   Remove the chicken from the oven and let it rest in the pan for a few minutes before transferring it to a cutting board. Separate the breast from the leg and slice the breast through the skin into a few pieces. Place a leg and the sliced breast on each of two plates, or divide the chicken among three plates. Surround with the Roasted Root Vegetables and drizzle the pan juices over all.

ROASTED ROOT VEGETABLES

SERVES 4

Using red pearl onions and purple potatoes gives this dish more color, but you can use white varieties of both. Because the vegetables will finish cooking at slightly different times, you may wish to keep them separated on the baking sheet; that way, if you want to remove, say, the carrots first, you can do it easily.

8 baby turnips, washed and dried

1 medium rutabaga, trimmed, peeled, and cut into 1-inch pieces

About 24 baby carrots, trimmed

8 purple Peruvian potatoes or any baby potatoes, washed and dried

1 cup peeled pearl onions, preferably red

3 tablespoons extra virgin olive oil

$1^1/2$ teaspoons kosher salt

2 fresh thyme sprigs

Heat the oven to 400°F. On a sided baking sheet large enough to hold the vegetables in a single layer, toss the vegetables with the olive oil, salt, and thyme. (You want a little space between the vegetables but not too much.) Roast the vegetables, stirring occasionally, until well browned in places and tender, about 40 minutes. Serve hot or warm.

RUSTIC BRAISED CHICKEN WITH SQUASH AND FRUIT PANZANELLA SERVES 4

The aroma from this chicken as it cooks is simply perfect. Every time I make it, I feel like I'm in a home kitchen in Italy. I like to take the chicken off the bone and serve it on the panzanella—mainly because it's easier to eat neatly—but you can serve it whole on the bone with the panzanella on the side, which would also be more in keeping with the title of this dish. Even better, substitute rabbit for the chicken.

1/4 cup extra virgin olive oil

4 skin-on chicken legs, excess fat and skin trimmed

Kosher salt and freshly ground black pepper

6 plum tomatoes, seeded and coarsely chopped

4 garlic cloves, crushed

3 small fresh rosemary sprigs

4 small fresh thyme sprigs

Pinch of crushed red pepper flakes

3/4 cup dry white wine

3 to 4 cups Chicken Broth (page 241)

Squash and Fruit Panzanella (recipe follows)

Four small handfuls baby greens, well washed and dried

BROWN THE CHICKEN   Heat 2 tablespoons of the olive oil in a very large ovenproof sauté pan over medium-high heat. Season the chicken with salt and pepper, add it to the pan, and brown it well on both sides, 8 to 10 minutes. (You may need to do this in batches depending on your pan and the size of the legs.) Remove the chicken from the pan, discard the oil, and wipe the pan with a paper towel.

BRAISE THE CHICKEN   Heat the oven to 325°F. Put the remaining 2 tablespoons olive oil in the pan and heat it over medium-high heat. Add the tomatoes, garlic, rosemary, thyme, and red pepper flakes. Cook, stirring, for a minute. Add the wine and continue to cook, stirring occasionally, until the wine has reduced by half, 7 to 8 minutes. Return the chicken to the pan and add the broth; it should come about two-thirds of the way up the sides of the chicken. Cover the pan with a lid or foil and cook in the oven until extremely tender, 1 hour and 10 minutes. Remove the chicken from the pan. Degrease the braising liquid and strain it. When the meat is cool enough to handle, remove it in large pieces from the bone, discarding the skin. (The chicken can be braised up to 2 days ahead. Refrigerate it and the braising liquid separately; this way you can easily remove the fat when it hardens.)

TO SERVE   Spoon off any visible fat from the braising liquid. Heat the liquid over medium-high heat and cook until reduced slightly, 5 to 10 minutes. Lower the heat to medium and add the chicken to the liquid to reheat it. Divide the Squash and Fruit Panzanella among four plates, piling it in the middle. Drizzle the panzanella with some of the chicken braising liquid. Top with the chicken pieces and more of the braising liquid. Garnish with a small handful of undressed baby greens and serve.

SQUASH AND FRUIT PANZANELLA

SERVES 4

When you think of panzanella (if you do at all) you probably think of the more classic additions to this bread salad: olives, tomatoes, basil, and olive oil. I love to play with the notion of panzanella, tailoring it to fit the main course. This is a favorite; I hope you love the combination of the squash, prunes, walnut oil, and fruit bread as much as I do. (If so, you may want to double it and serve it with a turkey on Thanksgiving.) You can make the various elements for the panzanella ahead of time, but don't mix them with the vinaigrette until shortly before serving.

2 tablespoons finely chopped prunes

$^1/_4$ cup red wine

1 small butternut squash or pumpkin

$^1/_4$ cup plus 2 tablespoons extra virgin olive oil

2 small fresh thyme sprigs

Pinch of crushed red pepper flakes

Kosher salt and freshly ground black pepper

3 to 4 slices fruit-studded bread, such as currant, raisin, or
    apricot (it's fine if it has nuts; see page 238 if you're feeling
    ambitious and want to make the bread yourself)

$^1/_4$ cup toasted walnut oil

1 tablespoon balsamic vinegar

1 tablespoon red wine vinegar   *(continued)*

STEEP THE PRUNES   Combine the prunes and wine in a small bowl and soak for at least 20 minutes.

ROAST THE SQUASH   Heat the oven to 400°F. Trim, peel, and seed the squash. Cut it into small (⅓-inch) cubes to yield about 2 cups (save any extra to add to a pasta or green salad). On a small sheet pan, toss the squash with a tablespoon or two of olive oil, the thyme, and the red pepper flakes. Season with salt and pepper and roast until browned and tender but still holding its shape, about 10 minutes.

CREATE THE CROUTONS   Trim the crusts from the bread and discard. Toast the slices under a broiler or on a grill until golden brown. Cut into ⅓-inch cubes to yield about 2 cups.

MAKE A VINAIGRETTE   In a medium bowl, whisk together the walnut oil, remaining ¼ cup olive oil, balsamic vinegar, and red wine vinegar. Season to taste with salt and pepper. Add the croutons and roasted squash and toss. Drain the prunes, add them, and toss well to combine. Serve soon after tossing.

CHICKEN LEGS WITH CUMIN SERVES 4

In this one-pan dish, the chicken and vegetables are cooked together in a very hot oven. With just the little bit of liquid in the pan, the favas will darken dramatically, the onions will begin to crisp, and the tomatoes will become almost "sun-dried." These are all good transformations, sure signals that flavors have intensified.

Heat the oven to 400°F.

BROWN THE CHICKEN   In a wide, heavy-based ovenproof sauté or frying pan, preferably cast iron, heat the oil over medium-high heat. Season the chicken parts well with salt and a lot of black pepper. Add the chicken, skin side down, and cook until the skin is well browned and crisp, about 10 minutes. Turn the chicken and crisp the other side for about 8 minutes.

TO FINISH   Add the onions, tomatoes, fava beans, and lemon juice to the pan. Sprinkle the cumin and red pepper flakes over all and bake, uncovered, until the chicken is done, 30 to 35 minutes. (The juices from a thigh piece will run clear when pricked with a fork.)

TO SERVE   Remove the chicken and vegetables from the oven and sprinkle with the parsley. Divide among four warm plates and serve immediately.

2 tablespoons extra virgin olive oil

3 to 3^1/$_2$ pounds chicken legs and thighs, with skin

Kosher salt and freshly ground black pepper

3 medium onions, cut in half through the root, each half cut into 4 wedges

1 pint cherry tomatoes, cut in half

1 cup fava beans, lima beans, or edamame

^{1}/$_2$ cup fresh lemon juice

^{1}/$_2$ teaspoon ground cumin

Pinch of crushed red pepper flakes

1 small bunch parsley, tough stems trimmed, well washed and dried

OLIVE OIL-POACHED CHICKEN BREAST WITH SAUTÉED BROCCOLI RABE AND HORSERADISH SAUCE SERVES 4

Because chicken is so lean, it takes very well to this method of cooking. What oil is absorbed makes the chicken lusciously silken.

1¹/2 to 2 cups extra virgin olive oil

1 shallot, halved and thinly sliced lengthwise

4 thin lemon slices

3 small fresh thyme sprigs

1 small fresh rosemary sprig

Generous pinch of crushed red pepper flakes

1 garlic clove, coarsely chopped

4 boneless, skinless chicken breasts, trimmed and thicker part butterflied to make evenly thick

Kosher salt and freshly ground black pepper

Sautéed Broccoli Rabe (recipe follows)

Potato Horseradish Sauce (recipe follows)

POACH THE CHICKEN   Heat 1½ cups of the olive oil, the shallot, lemon, thyme, rosemary, red pepper flakes, and garlic in a high-sided sauté pan over medium-low heat. When the aromatics begin to sizzle, take the pan off the heat and let them steep in the oil for 10 to 15 minutes. Return the pan to medium low. Season the chicken with a little salt and pepper and then slide it into the hot oil. It should be about three-quarters submerged; add more oil if needed. Let the chicken cook slowly, turning it once or twice during cooking, until it is mostly opaque with just a little pink, about 10 minutes. Remove from heat and let the chicken finish cooking in the pan's residual heat.

TO SERVE   Slice the warm chicken. Divide the broccoli rabe among four plates, top with the chicken slices, and drizzle each serving with a couple tablespoons of the horseradish sauce.

SAUTÉED BROCCOLI RABE

SERVES 4

Kosher salt

1 bunch broccoli rabe (about 1 pound), trimmed of
    tough stems and rinsed well

2 tablespoons extra virgin olive oil

3 shallots, halved and thinly sliced lengthwise

COOK THE BROCCOLI RABE   Bring a medium saucepan of well-salted water to a boil. Add the broccoli rabe and cook until just tender, about 5 minutes. Drain well.

CARAMELIZE THE SHALLOTS   Heat the olive oil in a medium sauté pan over medium heat. Add the shallots, season with a little salt, and cook, stirring occasionally, until tender and well browned, 10 to 12 minutes.

TO FINISH   Add the rabe to the pan with the shallots, stir to combine, and keep warm until ready to serve.

A very versatile side dish.

POTATO HORSERADISH SAUCE

MAKES ABOUT 1^1/$_2$ CUPS

I try to stay far away from cream in my kitchen. Using it too often feels like a cop-out to me. Sometimes my chefs sneak a little cream into this sauce, but I like it made "creamy" by an olive oil emulsion instead so the horseradish flavor is not obscured. This sauce would also be delicious with seared salmon.

^{1}/$_2$ medium horseradish root (about 2^1/$_2$ ounces), peeled and coarsely grated

^{1}/$_2$ cup Chicken Broth (page 241)

1 small Yukon gold potato (about 4 ounces), peeled and cut into large chunks

Kosher salt

3 tablespoons extra virgin olive oil

MAKE THE HORSERADISH JUICE   In a blender, puree the horseradish with the chicken broth. Strain through a fine mesh strainer into a bowl and reserve the liquid.

COOK THE POTATOES   Place the potato in a small saucepan with cold salted water to cover by 2 inches and bring to a boil. Cook until tender, about 5 minutes. Remove the potato from the pan, but keep the cooking water.

MAKE THE SAUCE   With a blender, puree the potato with ½ cup of the potato cooking water. With the blender on, add the oil in a thin stream. Next add the horseradish juice; the sauce should have a thick cream consistency and a strong horseradish taste. Season to taste with salt. If not using right away, refrigerate for up to 3 days and reheat gently.

GRILLED CHICKEN WITH CHARRED LEMON AND HEIRLOOM TOMATOES SERVES 4 TO 6

Maybe it's my suburban upbringing, but I don't really feel like summer has come until I see flames shoot out from the barbecue and smell the distinct aroma of chicken charring. That smell means I'm going to get my grilled chicken the way I like it, with some of the pieces quite blackened. I may not want to eat the burned skin per se, but I know the meat underneath is going to taste smoky and delicious.

MARINATE THE CHICKEN Combine 1 cup of the olive oil, the lemon, scallions, onions, and red pepper flakes in a large bowl or large zip-top bag. Add the chicken pieces and toss to coat. Marinate for at least a few hours, refrigerated.

GRILL THE CHICKEN Prepare the coals on an outdoor grill to medium-hot or heat a gas grill. (If using coals, bank them to one side of the grill so that one side is hot and the other less so.) Season the chicken pieces well with salt and pepper, then lay them on the grill along with the onions, scallions, and lemon slices. Put the cover on the grill to increase the heat and cook the hell out of the chicken. The grill will smoke like crazy, but try to resist opening the lid for 7 minutes or so. When you do, turn the chicken pieces and continue cooking, most of the time with the lid on, until done, about 35 minutes. If the chicken, lemon, and onions are getting too charred, reduce the heat or move them to a cooler part of the grill.

MAKE A VINAIGRETTE Meanwhile, finely chop the anchovies, if using. Combine them with the vinegar, the ¼ cup olive oil, and the parsley, and whisk well.

TO SERVE Brush the bread with olive oil and grill on both sides. Divide the chicken, lemon, scallions, and onions among serving plates. Put the tomato wedges alongside and drizzle with the vinaigrette. Serve with the grilled bread.

1¼ cups extra virgin olive oil, plus more for brushing the bread

1 lemon, sliced

2 bunches scallions, roots trimmed

2 medium onions, thickly sliced

1 or 2 pinches of crushed red pepper flakes

2 chickens, cut into pieces

Kosher salt and freshly ground black pepper

2 to 3 anchovy fillets, well rinsed (optional)

1 tablespoon red wine vinegar

½ cup chopped fresh parsley

4 to 6 slices ciabatta bread

6 to 8 medium, very ripe heirloom tomatoes or juicy beefsteak tomatoes, cut into wedges

GRILLED QUAIL WITH SHALLOTS, GRAPES, WALNUTS, AND CREAMY POLENTA SERVES 4

When you buy quail, they come already partially boned, so despite their being a little exotic, they're actually quite easy to prepare. (You could, however, substitute butterflied Cornish hens—serve a half hen per person—if you increase the overall cooking time and temperature and cook them through.) I like to grill quail, but you could also sear them in batches in a heavy-based sauté pan. Finishing quail in a very low oven relaxes the meat, making it extremely tender. Have the polenta cooking for a while before beginning the quail.

1^1/$_2$ tablespoons extra virgin olive oil, plus more for rubbing the quail

5 medium shallots, thinly sliced

1 cup quartered red seedless grapes

^{1}/$_4$ cup toasted walnuts, broken into pieces

8 partially boned quail

Kosher salt and freshly ground black pepper

Creamy Polenta (recipe follows)

PREPARE THE GRAPES AND WALNUTS   In a large sauté pan, heat 1 tablespoon of the olive oil over medium heat. Add the shallots and cook, stirring occasionally and adding more oil if needed, until tender and browned, about 15 minutes. Add the grapes, increase the heat a little, and cook until the grapes release much of their liquid (some of it will cook off), about 5 minutes. Add the walnuts and reserve off the heat.

COOK THE QUAIL   Heat the oven to 225°F. Prepare an outdoor grill to medium-hot or heat an indoor grill pan over medium-high heat. Rub the quail all over with olive oil and season well with salt and pepper. Have a sided baking sheet nearby for finishing the quail. Grill the quail, turning once, about 5 minutes per side for rare to medium-rare. Transfer the quail to the baking sheet and let them sit in the warm oven for 10 minutes to rest before serving. (Note: If you're cooking Cornish hens, they will need to finish cooking in the oven after the initial sear. In that case, increase the heat to 300°F and cook until the juices of the thigh run clear when pierced, about 40 minutes.)

TO SERVE   Reheat the grapes and walnuts, if necessary. Divide the polenta among four warm serving plates. Top with the grape-walnut mixture and then the quail. Serve immediately.

CREAMY POLENTA

SERVES 4 TO 6

This polenta is so good I have to restrain myself from serving it with everything. If you are in a hurry, you can serve it after less than an hour of simmering, but its texture becomes its supple best with a little more cooking time.

2 cups heavy cream

2 cups milk

1^1/$_2$ teaspoons kosher salt, or more to taste

^{2}/$_3$ cup cornmeal, preferably coarse

1 tablespoon unsalted butter

2 tablespoons grated grana Padano or Parmigiano-Reggiano

1 teaspoon chopped fresh chives (optional)

In a heavy-based saucepan, combine the cream and milk and heat over medium-high heat just until small bubbles begin to appear on the surface. Add the salt and whisk until quite frothy.

Add the cornmeal and continue to whisk the mixture as it comes to a boil. Continue whisking for an additional 3 minutes. Reduce the heat to very low, cover the pan, and cook, stirring every 10 minutes or so, until the cornmeal is completely cooked and quite tender, about 1½ hours. As the polenta cooks, a skin will form on the bottom and sides of the pan (unless you are using a nonstick pan); this is proper and gives the polenta a slightly toasty flavor.

Just before serving, stir in the butter, cheese, and chives, if using. Season to taste with salt. The polenta should pour from the spoon as you serve it and will thicken as it cools. If necessary, you can thin the polenta with a little milk just before serving. Divide the polenta among heated bowls or plates.

BRAISED RABBIT WITH HERBED SPAETZLE, CARAMELIZED PARSNIPS, AND MINT SERVES 4

People respond to this dish with unabashed joy when it's on the menu. I think it has a lot to do with the mint; it brightens the plate as well as the mood, a reminder not to take everything so seriously. If you can't find rabbit legs or object to eating rabbit on the basis of it being cuter than chicken, substitute the same number of bone-in chicken thighs; the cooking time will be less, however.

5 tablespoons extra virgin olive oil

6 rabbit hind legs

Kosher salt and freshly ground black pepper

6 plum tomatoes, seeded and coarsely chopped

2 garlic cloves, crushed

4 small fresh rosemary sprigs

2 to 3 cups Chicken Reduction (page 242) or good-quality purchased chicken base, reconstituted as the package directs until a little thicker than chicken broth

1 medium parsnip, very finely diced

Herbed Spaetzle (recipe follows)

1 tablespoon finely chopped fresh mint

Finely chopped fresh parsley (optional)

BROWN THE RABBIT   In a large ovenproof sauté pan, heat 2 tablespoons of the olive oil over medium-high heat. Season the rabbit legs with salt and pepper and brown them well on both sides, about 8 minutes. Remove the legs from the pan, discard the oil, and wipe the pan with a paper towel.

BRAISE THE RABBIT   Heat the oven to 325°F. Put 2 tablespoons of the olive oil in the pan and heat it over medium-high heat. Add the tomatoes, garlic, and rosemary. Cook, stirring, for a minute. Return the legs to the pan and add the chicken reduction; it should come about two-thirds of the way up the sides of the legs. Cover the pan with a lid or foil and cook in the oven until extremely tender, 1 hour and 10 minutes. Remove the legs from the pan, degrease the braising liquid, if necessary, and strain it. When the meat is cool enough to handle, take it off the bone. (The rabbit can be braised up to 2 days ahead; refrigerate the meat and the braising liquid separately.)

TO FINISH   Simmer the braising liquid over medium-high heat until it reduces slightly, 5 to 10 minutes. Lower the heat to medium-low, add the rabbit meat, and gently reheat it.

Meanwhile, heat a tablespoon of olive oil in a small sauté pan over medium-high heat. Add the parsnip and cook, stirring, until just tender and browned. Add the parsnip and a few spoonfuls of the braising liquid to the browned Herbed Spaetzle and heat briefly together. Add the mint to the rabbit in the pan and give it a quick stir. Divide the spaetzle among four plates and top with the rabbit meat as well as some of the sauce. Garnish with a little parsley, if you like.

HERBED SPAETZLE

SERVES 4

The addition of herbs makes spaetzle attractively speckled. I did not add a lot of herbs because of the mint in the rabbit recipe this is paired with. If you're serving the spaetzle with something else and want more herb flavor, double the amount. If you don't have all three of the herbs, you can use any two. A single herb, however, would overwhelm.

2 large eggs

3/4 to 1 cup milk

1 teaspoon finely chopped fresh chives

1 teaspoon finely chopped fresh parsley

1 teaspoon finely chopped fresh thyme

Kosher salt and freshly ground black pepper

2 cups all-purpose flour, plus more if needed

2 tablespoons extra virgin olive oil, plus more for drizzling

2 tablespoons unsalted butter

(continued)

MAKE THE SPAETZLE BATTER   In a bowl, whisk together the eggs, ¾ cup milk, and the herbs. Season with a good pinch of salt and pepper. Add the flour and beat well until combined. If the dough is very wet, add more flour a tablespoon at a time; if dry, add a little milk.

BOIL THE SPAETZLE   Bring a pot of salted water to a boil. In batches, press the spaetzle batter through the holes of a colander or through the large slots on a box grater, letting the irregularly shaped dumplings drop into the boiling water.

With a slotted spoon or sieve, scoop out the spaetzle when cooked (they will float) and transfer to a baking sheet. Drizzle the spaetzle with a little olive oil to prevent them from sticking to each other. Repeat until you have used up all the batter. (You can make the spaetzle up to a day before serving; keep the spaetzle refrigerated.)

TO SERVE   Heat a large sauté pan over medium-high heat. Add the butter and a couple tablespoons of olive oil. Add the spaetzle and cook until golden brown, about 2 minutes.

MEAT

My approach to cooking most meat is to give it a quick sear for color and flavor and then finish in a very low oven. This method requires a little patience, but the result is meat cooked to tender perfection, the doneness that you like throughout. The reason is that the low heat lets the muscle, which contracted mightily when it hit the hot pan, relax a little. Though it takes a little longer, this method cuts down on the post-cooking resting time for the meat, which allows for the redistribution of the juices.

If meltingly tender meat is what you're after, however, turn to the braises in this chapter, such as the short ribs on page 187 or the beef stew on page 192. Always braise meat until fork-tender and just about falling off the bone. (Better that the meat on a short rib actually comes off the bone rather than tenaciously clings to it; the more stubbornly it holds, the tougher the meat will be.) Braises and stews are easier to degrease after being thoroughly cooled (the fat rises to the surface and solidifies), which is a good reason to make them a day or two before serving. The flavor will improve in that time, too.

SPICE-COATED PORK LOIN WITH BUTTERNUT SQUASH AND WILTED ARUGULA SERVES 6

If you don't have two ovens, roast the squash first, let it stand at room temperature while the pork roasts, and then reheat the squash during the ten minutes or so the pork needs to rest before slicing.

4 teaspoons cumin seeds

1 teaspoon whole cloves

1 teaspoon black peppercorns

1 teaspoon mustard seeds

1 teaspoon ground cinnamon

4 teaspoons paprika

1 tablespoon plus 1 teaspoon salt

One 3- to 3^1/$_3$-pound boneless, center-cut pork loin

^{1}/$_4$ cup extra virgin olive oil

2 bunches arugula, well washed and dried, tough stems removed

Sweet and Spicy Roasted Butternut Squash (recipe follows)

Sea salt

FOR THE SPICE MIX   In a small sauté pan, heat the whole spices (cumin, cloves, peppercorns, and mustard) over low heat, occasionally stirring with a wooden spoon to prevent scorching, until quite fragrant, 5 to 8 minutes. Add the cinnamon and paprika and cook for an additional minute. Allow the spices to cool for a few minutes and then grind them coarsely in a spice grinder or coffee grinder dedicated to spices. Mix in the salt. The spice mix, which makes about ½ cup, will keep for at least a month if tightly covered.

MARINATE THE PORK   Cut the pork loin in two pieces crosswise. Rub the pork all over with about a tablespoon of olive oil and then coat it with about half of the spice mix. A good way to get an even coating is to sprinkle the spice rub on a cutting board and roll the loin over the spices. Wrap the pork well in plastic and let it marinate for a half hour at room temperature or in the refrigerator for up to 24 hours.

SLOW-ROAST THE PORK   Heat the oven to 250°F. Remove the pork from the plastic wrap and lightly pat dry if needed. Heat a large ovenproof sauté pan over medium-high heat and add enough olive

The spice rub used on this pork will fill your kitchen with a wonderfully warm fragrance.

oil to coat the bottom, about 2 tablespoons. Add the pork and brown it well on all sides, about 5 minutes. Transfer the pan to the oven and cook until a thermometer inserted diagonally at least 2 inches into the pork registers 155°F, about 45 minutes. Let stand, loosely covered, for 10 minutes before slicing.

WILT THE ARUGULA   While the pork rests, heat the remaining 1 tablespoon of olive oil in a large sauté pan over medium heat. Add the arugula and cook, stirring, just until wilted, then keep warm.

TO SERVE   Place a round of the squash off to one side of the plate. Divide the arugula among the plates, placing it near the squash and toward the other side of the plate. Slice the pork loin and lay the slices on the arugula, near and slightly overlapping the squash. Finish with a tiny pinch of sea salt and serve.

SWEET AND SPICY ROASTED BUTTERNUT SQUASH

SERVES 6

If you would like to make this squash and have not made the spice rub that goes along with the pork loin in the preceding recipe, simply combine a half teaspoon of paprika, a quarter teaspoon of ground cumin, and a pinch each of ground cloves, mustard, and cinnamon. In place of the butternut squash, you could use acorn squash or kabocha.

1 tablespoon extra virgin olive oil

1 medium butternut squash, neck peeled and cut into six $^1/_2$-inch slices (save the rest of the squash for another use)

Kosher salt and freshly ground black pepper

2 teaspoons unsalted butter

1 teaspoon spice mix from Spice-Coated Pork Loin (preceding recipe)

1 teaspoon dark brown sugar

Heat the oven to 350°F. Heat the olive oil in a large ovenproof sauté pan over medium heat. Add the squash, season with salt and pepper, and brown lightly on one side, about 5 minutes. Take the pan off the heat. Turn the squash over and dot it with the butter. Sprinkle the spice mix and the brown sugar evenly over the slices and finish cooking in the oven until the slices are tender, about 15 minutes.

SAUSAGE AND POLENTA RAGU SERVES 4 TO 6

I like to serve a tiny bit of this ragu alongside some grilled quail. But you probably don't eat like that at home, right? That's okay, because it can also be a very tasty, very casual-feeling meal on its own. I like it best when the polenta has firmed up a bit, but not enough to keep the sausage from sinking into it a little.

MAKE THE POLENTA Lightly grease a 2-quart baking or gratin dish. In a large pot, bring 2 cups water and the milk to a boil. Whisk in the 1½ teaspoons salt and the cornmeal and cook, still whisking, for a couple of minutes. Reduce the heat to low and cook, stirring occasionally, until the polenta has thickened and become tender, 30 to 45 minutes. Spoon all of the polenta into the prepared dish. (You want to make the polenta ahead of the topping so that it firms up a little. You can even make it a day ahead and refrigerate it, but let it come to room temperature before baking.)

COOK THE SAUSAGE TOPPING Meanwhile, heat the olive oil in a large sauté pan over medium-high heat. Add the onion, season with a generous pinch of salt, and cook, stirring, until lightly browned. Add the sausage and cook, using a wooden spoon to break up the meat, until most of the pinkness is gone. Add the tomatoes and cook another couple of minutes. Season to taste with salt and remove from the heat.

TO SERVE Heat the oven to 350°F. If the polenta is still hot, let it cool just enough so that the edges begin to firm up, about 15 minutes. Sprinkle the sausage and onion mixture over the polenta and bake for 20 minutes. Sprinkle the cheese over all, bake another 5 minutes, and serve.

2 cups milk

1½ teaspoons kosher salt, plus more for seasoning

1 cup cornmeal, preferably coarse

2 tablespoons olive oil

1 onion, cut into a medium dice

¾ pound Italian sausage, ideally half hot and half sweet, removed from its casing

3 plum tomatoes, cut into a medium dice

2 tablespoons grated grana Padano or Parmigiano-Reggiano

BRAISED SPARERIBS WITH TYROLEAN POTATOES AND ARTICHOKES SERVES 4

Braising spareribs makes them almost ridiculously tender. Though the deeply flavored sauce means these are a little messy to eat by hand, you will not be able to resist picking the ribs up to gnaw on every last bit. Delicious with the potatoes that follow, an even easier accompaniment would be pasta tossed with some of the braising liquid and topped with a little cheese and fresh parsley.

4 pounds pork spareribs, cut into individual ribs

Kosher salt and freshly ground black pepper

1 tablespoon plus 1 teaspoon ground cumin

2 to 3 tablespoons extra virgin olive oil

1 small carrot, diced

1 celery stalk, diced

1 medium onion, chopped

4 garlic cloves, coarsely chopped

1 cup dry white wine

1/2 cup red wine vinegar

6 plum tomatoes, seeded and cut into eighths

2 cups Chicken Reduction (page 242) or good-quality purchased chicken base, reconstituted as the package directs until a little thicker than chicken broth

3 small fresh thyme sprigs

3 small fresh rosemary sprigs

Tyrolean Potatoes and Artichokes (recipe follows)

BROWN THE RIBS   Heat the oven to 300°F. Season the spareribs all over with salt and pepper and rub with the tablespoon of cumin. Heat 2 tablespoons of olive oil in a deep, heavy-based ovenproof pan or Dutch oven over medium-high heat. Working in batches, brown the ribs on all sides, then transfer them to a bowl or platter.

BRAISE THE RIBS   Add the carrot, celery, onion, and garlic to the pan with more olive oil if necessary. Sauté the vegetables until browned. Stir in the teaspoon of cumin and cook another minute or two. Add the wine and vinegar and bring to a boil, scraping up the bits stuck to the bottom of the pan. Continue to cook until the liquid is reduced by about one-third. Add the tomatoes, the chicken reduction, the thyme and rosemary, and the seared ribs with any accumulated juices. Bring to a boil, cover the pot, and transfer the ribs to the oven, turning them a few times during cooking, until fork-tender and the meat is just barely clinging to the bone, 2 to 2½ hours.

DEGREASE AND REDUCE THE SAUCE   Remove the ribs from the sauce and strain the cooking liquid. If you are serving the ribs right away, keep them warm. Use a large spoon or ladle to remove as much of the clear fat floating on top of the cooking liquid as possible, then cook the defatted sauce over medium-high heat until it reduces somewhat, becoming thicker and more flavorful. If making the ribs ahead, refrigerate them in their cooking liquid and then remove the hardened fat on top. Reheat the ribs in a 300°F oven in the cooking liquid. This reheating may reduce the sauce enough; if not, remove the ribs and cook it down until thicker and more flavorful.

TO SERVE   Serve a pile of ribs drizzled with some of the sauce next to a serving of the Tyrolean Potatoes and Artichokes.

TYROLEAN POTATOES AND ARTICHOKES
SERVES 4

These potatoes are inspired by ones I ate in Alto Adige, which is also called Südtirol.

6 large fingerling potatoes

$1/4$ teaspoon kosher salt

3 tablespoons extra virgin olive oil

1 artichoke, trimmed, choke removed, and sliced very thin

2 shallots, halved and thinly sliced lengthwise

$1^1/2$ ounces thinly sliced pancetta, chopped

2 to 3 tablespoons chicken broth

$1/2$ teaspoon chopped fresh chives

BLANCH THE POTATOES   Boil the potatoes whole in their skins in salted water until no longer hard but still a bit resistant when pierced with a knife. Drain, cool, and slice into ½-inch rounds.

SAUTÉ THE POTATOES AND ARTICHOKE   Heat the olive oil over medium-high heat in a large sauté pan. Add the potatoes, season with the salt, and cook, stirring occasionally, until lightly browned, 3 to 4 minutes. Add the artichoke, shallots, and pancetta, and continue to cook until the potatoes and artichoke are tender and well browned, about 10 minutes. Add a little chicken broth if the vegetables stick to the pan. Sprinkle with the chives and serve immediately.

RIB EYE OF BEEF WITH KALE AND BLUEFOOT MUSHROOMS SERVES 4

My favorite way to cook a steak is to briefly sear the outside before letting it cook gently and relatively slowly in a low oven. You wind up with a beautiful piece of medium-rare meat that's the same color throughout (not just a little reddish in its center). By transferring the steak to a clean pan to finish cooking, I can use the oil mingling with the steak's own juices as a sort of sauce, without worrying that the oil has scorched in a hot pan. An added benefit of this style of cooking is that you can get the rest of the meal prepared in the twenty minutes or so the meat spends unattended in the oven. Nice.

SEAR THE BEEF Heat the oven to 225°F. Put 3 tablespoons of the olive oil, the rosemary, and the garlic in a large ovenproof sauté pan and set aside. Coat the steaks lightly with olive oil and season both sides with salt and a little pepper. If the steaks are very cold, allow them to warm up a bit at room temperature before cooking.

If you have a grill on your stove or easy access to an outdoor grill, heat the grill to medium hot and grill the steaks just so the exterior of the meat is nicely browned. If you don't have a grill, sear the meat on both sides in a heavy-based sauté pan (*not* the prepared pan) over medium-high heat. The entire browning process should last no more than 4 minutes for a thick cut of beef and a little less for thinner cuts. Transfer the steak to the prepared pan.

FINISH IN THE OVEN Put the pan in the oven and baste the meat with the olive oil every 4 to 5 minutes, until the meat is cooked to your liking, 18 to 20 minutes for medium rare (130°F on a meat thermometer). Check the thinner cuts earlier. Transfer the steak to a cutting board to rest for at least 5 minutes before slicing, but reserve the meat juices and the olive oil in the pan.

TO SERVE Briefly reheat the reserved oil and juices. Divide the kale and Bluefoot Mushrooms among four warm plates. Slice the

3 tablespoons extra virgin olive oil, plus more for rubbing the steak

2 small fresh rosemary sprigs

2 garlic cloves, sliced paper-thin

1 1/2 to 2 pounds rib eye steak (1 or 2 steaks), preferably dry-aged and at least 1 1/2 inches thick

Kosher salt and freshly ground black pepper

Kale and Bluefoot Mushrooms (recipe follows)

1/2 teaspoon truffle oil

Pinch of sea salt

1 ounce Parmigiano-Reggiano

beef across the grain and lay over the kale. Stir the truffle oil into the reserved oil and juices and immediately drizzle a little over the meat. Sprinkle a bit of sea salt over each plate. Use a vegetable peeler to thinly shave the Parmigiano over the beef. Serve immediately.

KALE AND BLUEFOOT MUSHROOMS
SERVES 4

Kale is a favorite green in Italy, one that's underused here. If you can find black kale, also called Tuscan kale, use it here, as it becomes very tender quickly; the frilly blue-green variety may need more cooking time. Sometimes for lunch, I'll skip the steak this is usually served with and just scramble a couple of eggs right in the pan with the kale and mushrooms.

$^1/_4$ cup extra virgin olive oil

2 large shallots, thinly sliced (about $^1/_2$ cup)

Kosher salt and freshly ground black pepper

7 ounces wild mushrooms (I like bluefoots), cleaned, trimmed, and sliced or broken into 1-inch pieces (about 2 cups)

12 ounces kale, preferably Tuscan, stemmed, well washed and dried, and coarsely chopped (about 5 cups)

In a large sauté pan, heat the olive oil over medium heat. Add the shallots, season with a pinch of salt, and cook, stirring occasionally, until tender and lightly browned, about 8 minutes. Add the mushrooms, increase the heat to medium-high, and cook, stirring occasionally, until the mushrooms begin to brown. Add the kale, season with salt and pepper, and cook, stirring occasionally and adjusting the heat as necessary, until the kale is tender, about 10 minutes. Reserve off the heat. Just before serving, set the pan over high heat to evaporate some of the juices and to reheat.

SHORT RIBS AND FREGOLA WITH CORN AND BUTTERNUT SQUASH SERVES 4

Short ribs not only can be made a couple of days ahead, but they also taste better for it. Be sure to cook the ribs fully for the most tender results; the meat should come easily off the bone with a fork.

BROWN THE RIBS Heat the oven to 300°F. Season the ribs all over with salt and pepper. Heat 2 tablespoons of olive oil in a deep, heavy-based Dutch oven or similar ovenproof pot over medium-high heat. Sear the ribs—in two batches if they don't fit in the pot in a single layer—until well browned all over.

BRAISE THE RIBS Remove the ribs and add the carrot, celery, onion, and garlic to the pot with more olive oil if necessary. Cook the vegetables, stirring, until browned. Add the wine and vinegar and, using a wooden spoon, scrape up the bits stuck to the bottom of the pan. Continue to cook until the liquid is reduced by about one-third. Add the tomatoes, the chicken reduction, and the thyme and rosemary. Return the ribs to the pot, bring the liquid to a boil, cover the pot, and put it in the oven. Cook, turning the ribs once or twice, until they are fork-tender and the meat is just barely clinging to the bone, 3½ to 4 hours.

DEGREASE AND REDUCE THE SAUCE Remove the ribs from the sauce and strain the cooking liquid. If you are serving the ribs right away, keep them warm. Use a large spoon or ladle to remove as much of the clear fat floating on top of the cooking liquid as possible, then cook the defatted sauce over medium-high heat until it reduces somewhat, becoming thicker and more flavorful.

If making the ribs ahead, refrigerate them in their cooking liquid and then remove the hardened fat on top. Reheat the ribs in a 300°F oven in the cooking liquid. This reheating may reduce the sauce

3½ to 4 pounds beef short ribs

Kosher salt and freshly ground black pepper

2 to 3 tablespoons olive oil

1 small carrot, diced

1 celery stalk, diced

1 medium onion, chopped

4 garlic cloves, coarsely chopped

¾ cup red wine

½ cup red wine vinegar

6 plum tomatoes, seeded and quartered

2 cups Chicken Reduction (page 242) or good-quality purchased chicken base, reconstituted as the package directs until a little thicker than chicken broth

3 small fresh thyme sprigs

3 small fresh rosemary sprigs

Fregola with Corn and Butternut Squash (recipe follows)

2 tablespoons chopped fresh parsley (optional)

enough; if not, remove the ribs and cook it down until thicker and more flavorful.

TO SERVE   Either slice the ribs across the grain or serve them whole on top of the Fregola with Corn and Butternut Squash. Drizzle the sauce over all, sprinkle with parsley, if you like, and serve.

FREGOLA WITH CORN AND BUTTERNUT SQUASH   SERVES 4

A Sardinian specialty, fregola is a toasted pasta not unlike couscous. In fact, if you can't find fregola, you can easily substitute regular couscous or, even better, the larger Israeli couscous.

1 to 2 tablespoons olive oil

1 1/2 cups finely diced butternut squash (the squash should be about the same size as the corn kernels)

1 cup corn kernels

2 shallots, thinly sliced

2 small fresh thyme sprigs

Kosher salt and freshly ground black pepper

1 cup fregola, Israeli couscous, or regular couscous cooked until tender according to package directions

1 tablespoon chopped fresh parsley

Heat a large sauté pan over medium-high heat. Add about a tablespoon of olive oil and cook the squash, stirring occasionally, until tender and browned, 5 to 8 minutes. Add the corn, shallots, thyme, additional oil if needed, and a little salt and pepper. Continue to cook, stirring, until the shallots are tender, another 8 minutes. Toss the vegetables with the fregola, adding a bit more oil if it seems too dry. Season to taste, top with parsley, and serve.

BEEF TENDERLOIN WITH PEARL ONION AGRODOLCE AND SAUTÉED SUMMER VEGETABLES SERVES 6

You can make the sauce and sauté the accompanying vegetables while the tenderloin slowly finishes cooking.

MARINATE THE BEEF   In a shallow plate or zip-top bag, combine 2 tablespoons of the olive oil, the red pepper flakes, the sliced garlic, and a sprig of rosemary. Add the tenderloin and coat well with the marinade. Wrap the meat and aromatics in plastic and refrigerate for a few hours or up to 24 hours.

SEAR AND SLOW-ROAST THE BEEF   Heat the oven to 250°F. Add 2 tablespoons of the olive oil, the halved garlic cloves, and the remaining rosemary to a heavy-based ovenproof sauté pan or small roasting pan. Set this pan aside.

Remove the meat from the marinade and season it very lightly with salt and pepper. Heat another 2 tablespoons of olive oil in another large, heavy-based sauté pan (*not* the prepared one) over medium-high heat. Sear the beef on all sides until nicely browned, leaving each side undisturbed for a few minutes to get a nice crust.

(continued)

7 tablespoons extra virgin olive oil

Pinch of crushed red pepper flakes

3 garlic cloves, one clove sliced, the other two cut in half

3 fresh rosemary sprigs

One 2$\frac{1}{2}$- to 3-pound beef tenderloin roast, trimmed

Kosher salt and freshly ground black pepper

1 cup pearl onions, peeled

1 teaspoon sugar

1 tablespoon red wine vinegar

1 cup Chicken Broth (page 241)

Sautéed Summer Vegetables (recipe follows)

Transfer the meat to the sauté pan with the garlic and finish cooking it in the low oven, basting the meat with the olive oil every 5 minutes or so, until the beef is cooked to your liking. We serve ours medium rare (about 130°F on a meat thermometer), which takes 45 to 50 minutes.

MAKE THE AGRODOLCE   Heat a medium sauté pan over medium-high heat. Add the remaining tablespoon of olive oil and when hot, add the onions. Season lightly with salt and cook, stirring occasionally, until lightly browned, about 5 minutes. Add the sugar and let it caramelize for a few minutes, making the onions browner still. Add the vinegar and shake the pan to coat the onions well. Add the broth, cover, and cook until the onions are quite tender, about 7 minutes. Reserve off the heat.

TO SERVE   Transfer the tenderloin to a cutting board to rest, reserving the juices and olive oil in the pan. Reheat the agrodolce and the Sautéed Summer Vegetables. Divide the vegetables among six warm plates. Slice the beef across the grain about ¼ inch thick. Fan the slices out on the plate, slightly overlapping the vegetables. Reheat the pan juices and drizzle them over the meat and vegetables before finishing the plate with some of the onions and a drizzle of the agrodolce sauce.

SAUTÉED SUMMER VEGETABLES

SERVES 6

Since you're likely serving these vegetables with beef tenderloin (preceding recipe), take the time to make them look nice. Dice them uniformly or, even better, use a roll cut if you know how. To make the zucchini look pretty and hold its shape during cooking, slice off the entire rounded side lengthwise, $1/4$ to $1/3$ inch thick. Put the (skin-on) slices flat side down and slice them crosswise about $1/4$ inch thick. In the colder months, you can substitute blanched, quartered Brussels sprouts for the zucchini; in the spring, try snap peas.

2 tablespoons olive oil

$1^1/4$ cups roll cut or neatly diced baby carrots

$1^1/4$ cups thinly sliced zucchini

$1^1/4$ cups roll cut or neatly diced new or fingerling potatoes, blanched briefly

2 small fresh thyme sprigs

Pinch of crushed red pepper flakes

Kosher salt

$1/4$ cup Chicken Broth (page 241)

In a very large sauté pan (you want a lot of surface space to help the vegetables brown), heat the olive oil over medium-high heat. Add the carrots and cook, stirring occasionally, until light golden brown. Add the zucchini, potatoes, thyme, red pepper flakes, and a pinch of salt and cook, stirring occasionally, until the zucchini and potatoes are lightly browned, too. Add the chicken broth and cook until most of it has evaporated but the vegetables are nicely moist and tender. Season to taste with salt and serve.

SMOKY BEEF AND POTATO STEW WITH ZUCCHINI, CAULIFLOWER, SPINACH, AND FONTINA CHEESE SERVES 6 TO 8

This hearty beef stew is inspired by some of the goulashes I enjoyed while living in and touring around Germany. The vegetables in this version, however, are not your typical beef stew candidates. Instead of a bunch of root vegetables, which in most stews wind up tasting (not to mention looking and feeling) pretty much the same, these keep their own distinct personalities, adding a welcome variation of texture as well as unexpected (in a beef stew) flavor. If you know how to do a roll cut, go for it on the fingerling potatoes; your finished dish will look just a bit nicer.

2 to 3 tablespoons olive oil

$3^{1}/_{2}$ to 4 pounds boneless beef chuck, cut into $1^{1}/_{2}$-inch pieces

Kosher salt

2 large shallots, thinly sliced (about $^{2}/_{3}$ cup)

$1^{1}/_{2}$ tablespoons fresh thyme leaves

7 whole canned tomatoes

2 whole star anise

$^{3}/_{4}$ teaspoon smoked paprika (also called *pimentón*)

2 tablespoons red wine vinegar

1 quart Chicken Reduction (page 242) or good-quality purchased chicken base, reconstituted as the package directs until a little thicker than chicken broth

5 to 6 fingerling potatoes or 2 to 3 Yukon golds, cut into 1-inch pieces (about 2 cups)

SEAR THE BEEF In a large, high-sided ovenproof sauté pan or Dutch oven, heat a tablespoon of olive oil over medium-high heat. Season the beef with about a teaspoon of kosher salt. Add the beef to the pan in a single layer (you may have to do this in batches, adding more oil if needed, so as not to crowd the pan) and brown on all sides, 8 to 10 minutes. Remove the beef and wipe out any excess oil with a paper towel, leaving any browned bits on the bottom of the pan.

BRAISE THE BEEF Heat the oven to 350°F. Add another tablespoon of oil to the pan the beef was seared in, and set over medium heat. Add the shallots and cook, stirring occasionally, for 2 minutes. Add the thyme and continue cooking the shallots until well browned, another 8 minutes. Add the tomatoes, star anise, and paprika and cook, crushing the tomatoes with the spoon as you stir occasionally, until the pan looks almost dry, about 10 minutes. Add the vinegar and cook until the pan looks almost dry again, about 5 minutes. Add the chicken reduction and return the meat to the pan. Cover and cook in the oven for 1½ hours.

Serve this hearty stew with some grilled bread.

ADD THE VEGETABLES   After 1½ hours, stir the potatoes and cauliflower into the stew. (If the pot looks dry, add up to 2 cups of chicken broth.) Continue cooking until the meat is tender and the cauliflower and potatoes are just tender, another 40 minutes. Stir in the zucchini and spinach and cook until the zucchini is just tender, another 10 to 15 minutes. Season to taste with additional salt, if needed.

TO SERVE   Divide the stew among warm bowls and top each with a little grated fontina.

½ small head of cauliflower, cut into small florets (about 2 cups)

1 to 2 cups Chicken Broth (page 241), if needed

3 small zucchini, cut into a 1 by ¼-inch julienne (about 2 cups)

2 cups coarsely chopped spinach

6 to 8 ounces fontina cheese, grated

BREADED VEAL CHOPS AND RADICCHIO WITH PROSCIUTTO-BALSAMIC SAUCE SERVES 4

To play off the rather mild flavor of veal, I serve bitter radicchio topped with a sauce that's a little tangy, a little sweet, and a little salty. To coat the veal, I briefly pulse panko—the Japanese bread crumbs now at virtually every supermarket—in a small food processor. You can skip this step, but I think it makes the dish more refined. I prefer veal cooked until medium, not medium rare.

4 bone-in veal rib chops, preferably at least 1$\frac{1}{2}$ inches thick

Kosher salt and freshly ground black pepper

2 large eggs

1 cup all-purpose flour

1 cup fine dry bread crumbs

1 head radicchio, cut into 8 wedges

$\frac{1}{4}$ cup extra virgin olive oil, plus more if needed

$\frac{1}{2}$ cup julienned prosciutto (about 2$\frac{1}{2}$ ounces)

$\frac{1}{2}$ cup balsamic vinegar

$\frac{1}{2}$ cup grated or shaved ricotta salata

COAT THE CHOPS   Season the chops lightly with salt and pepper. Whisk the eggs together in a shallow bowl or pie plate. Put the flour on a plate and season it with salt and pepper. Set the bread crumbs on another plate. In assembly-line fashion, coat each chop with flour on both sides, dip it in the beaten eggs, then coat both sides with the bread crumbs. Refrigerate the chops for half an hour to an hour.

STEAM-ROAST THE RADICCHIO   Heat the oven to 350°F. Lay the radicchio wedges on a small sided baking sheet and drizzle with about 1½ tablespoons olive oil. Season with salt and pepper and cover the pan with aluminum foil. (Covering the pan allows the radicchio to steam and roast at the same time.) Cook until very tender and lightly browned, about 15 minutes. Remove from the oven and reserve on the baking sheet.

A breaded veal chop is simplicity itself.

MAKE THE SAUCE   In a small saucepan, heat 1½ teaspoons olive oil over medium-high heat. Add the prosciutto and cook, stirring, until well crisped, about 3 minutes. Pour off any excess oil, then add the vinegar. Boil the vinegar with the prosciutto until reduced by about a third and slightly thickened, about 3 minutes. Keep the sauce warm but off the heat.

SEAR AND SLOW-ROAST THE CHOPS   Heat the oven to 225°F. Heat the remaining 2 tablespoons olive oil over medium-high heat in a large ovenproof sauté pan. In batches, if necessary, sear the veal chops on both sides until well browned, adjusting the heat as needed to prevent the bread crumbs from burning. Transfer the chops to the low oven to slowly finish cooking, 15 to 30 minutes, depending on the thickness of the chops. They're done when the internal temperature reads 140°F to 145°F for medium. Let the veal rest at room temperature for 5 minutes before serving.

TO SERVE   Reheat the radicchio in the oven if necessary. Separate the radicchio leaves and pile them onto four warm plates, drizzle the balsamic sauce over the radicchio, and top with the ricotta salata. Place a veal chop alongside the pile and serve immediately.

GRILLED LAMB CHOPS WITH SMOKED PAPRIKA AND MINTED COUSCOUS SERVES 6

In this lamb dish, I use two kinds of paprika, one on each side of the lamb. This way, you get a bold smokiness that's not going to overwhelm the flavor of the meat. If you have a gas grill, you can cook the lamb completely on it. If you're cooking over coals, stack them to one side so you can sear the lamb over high heat before moving it to a cooler spot on the grill for indirect cooking. For even more control, finish cooking the lamb in a low oven.

12 thick loin or rib lamb chops, trimmed

2 tablespoons extra virgin olive oil, plus more for drizzling

1 tablespoon smoked paprika (also called *pimentón*)

1 tablespoon dark brown sugar

1 tablespoon sweet Hungarian paprika

1 tablespoon coarse sea salt

Minted Couscous with Almonds and Currants (recipe follows)

FLAVOR THE LAMB Coat the lamb chops well with 2 tablespoons of olive oil and lay them on a baking sheet. Sprinkle the smoked paprika evenly over one side. Sprinkle half of the brown sugar over that side as well. Turn the chops over and sprinkle the other side with the sweet paprika and the remaining brown sugar. Let sit for a half hour at room temperature or wrap in plastic and refrigerate for up to 24 hours.

GRILL THE LAMB Heat a grill (or, if cooking indoors, a large grill pan) until hot. If you plan to finish the lamb in the oven, heat it to 250°F; if using a coal grill, bank the hot coals to one side. Just before grilling, amply salt both sides of the lamb. Grill the chops over high heat until well browned, even lightly charred, on one side, about 3 minutes. Turn the lamb over and brown the other side for 1 or 2 minutes. If using a gas grill, reduce the heat to low. If using charcoal, move the lamb as far away from the coals as possible. (Or put the lamb on a sheet pan and finish it in the oven.) Continue cooking over low heat until the lamb registers medium rare (130°F to 135°F on a meat thermometer), about 5 minutes.

TO SERVE Divide the Minted Couscous among six plates or spoon onto a platter. Prop a couple of lamb chops against the couscous and drizzle a little olive oil as well as any lamb juices over the meat, and serve.

(continued)

MINTED COUSCOUS WITH ALMONDS AND CURRANTS

SERVES 6

This couscous goes really well with the rich smoky flavor of the lamb. If the almonds are toasted ahead of time, you can make the couscous start to finish while the lamb cooks. The couscous would also taste really good with the braised chicken on page 164.

2 teaspoons olive oil

1 tablespoon chopped shallot

$1/2$ teaspoon kosher salt, plus more for seasoning

1 cup couscous

$1^3/4$ cups Chicken Broth (page 241)

$1/3$ cup chopped toasted almonds

$1/3$ cup currants

$1/4$ cup chopped fresh mint, plus more for garnish (optional)

Heat the olive oil in a small saucepan over medium-high heat. Add the shallot and salt and cook for 1 minute. Add the couscous and the broth. Bring to a boil, cover, and take the pan off the heat. Let the couscous steam for 5 to 7 minutes. Fluff the couscous with a fork and stir in the almonds, currants, and mint. Season with additional salt, garnish with more mint, if you like, and serve.

GRILLED BUTTERFLIED LEG OF LAMB WITH TOMATO AND ARUGULA SALAD SERVES 6

One thing I really like about cooking a butterflied leg of lamb is that because its thickness varies, the slices of meat you bring to the table will vary in how well cooked they are. Unless all of your guests like lamb cooked to the exact same doneness, this is a good thing.

MARINATE THE LAMB   In a food processor or blender, combine the parsley, onions, garlic, and vinegar. Puree the ingredients while adding the olive oil in a stream. You want a loose puree, so add more oil if needed.

Season the lamb well with salt and pepper. Lay the lamb out flat and coat it all over with the parsley mixture. Allow the flavor of the marinade to penetrate for at least 1 hour at room temperature or up to 24 hours covered in plastic wrap and refrigerated.

GRILL THE LAMB   Prepare the grill of your choice to medium hot. Grill the lamb on one side for about 10 minutes. Turn the meat and cook until a thermometer inserted in the thickest part of the meat registers 130°F to 135°F for medium rare, another 10 to 15 minutes, depending on thickness. Transfer the meat to a cutting board and let it rest, loosely covered in aluminum foil, for 10 minutes.

TO SERVE   Carve the meat across the grain into thin slices. Fan the slices out on serving plates next to the Tomato and Arugula Salad.

(continued)

2 bunches parsley, well washed and dried, tough stems removed

1 cup "Pickled" Red Onions (page 69)

2 garlic cloves, coarsely chopped

1/4 cup red wine vinegar

1/2 cup extra virgin olive oil, plus more if needed

1 boneless butterflied leg of lamb, 4 to 5 pounds, well trimmed

Kosher salt and freshly ground black pepper

Tomato and Arugula Salad (recipe follows)

TOMATO AND ARUGULA SALAD
SERVES 6

This is a really pretty and easy way to feature two summer favorites: tomatoes and arugula. The combination of sweet tomatoes, peppery arugula, and tangy onions goes especially well with grilled lamb, although these would also look and taste terrific alongside a grilled rib eye or even marinated tuna steaks. Assemble and plate the salad while the meat rests.

4 large, ripe beefsteak tomatoes

1 bunch arugula, leaves only, well washed and dried, tough stems removed

4 to 5 tablespoon extra virgin olive oil

Sea salt or kosher salt

$1/2$ cup "Pickled" Red Onions (page 69)

Slice the tomatoes thickly to get 12 slices about the same size. Toss the arugula with a teaspoon or two of the olive oil, just enough to barely coat the leaves. Lay a slice of tomato on each plate. Drizzle each slice with a teaspoon of olive oil and sprinkle with a tiny pinch of salt. Lay some arugula leaves on each tomato slice and top with another tomato slice. Finish with more olive oil, more salt, and the onions.

MOIST-ROASTED LEG OF LAMB WITH EGGPLANT, TOMATOES, AND POTATOES SERVES 6 TO 8

I like to cook large pieces of meat using a method that's a mix of roasting and braising. I brown the meat in a little oil and then cook it uncovered in less liquid and in a hotter oven than I would use for an actual braise. I call this moist-roasting because the moisture in the oven makes the meat very tender, but the high temperature also browns the exposed meat, which adds a ton of flavor. The final texture of the meat, however, will be stewlike, so don't look for medium rare when you cook lamb this way; the meat should easily come off the bone when prodded by a fork.

MARINATE THE LAMB   Combine the ½ cup of olive oil, the rosemary, garlic, red pepper flakes, a teaspoon of salt, and a teaspoon of pepper. Rub the lamb all over with this mixture and then wrap it in plastic. Marinate the lamb for at least a few hours, refrigerated and preferably overnight.

PREPARE THE EGGPLANT   Put the eggplant in a colander and toss with 1 teaspoon salt. Put the colander in a clean sink, weight the eggplant, and allow the salt to draw out the excess moisture for 30 minutes.

MOIST-ROAST THE LAMB   Heat the oven to 400°F. In a heavy-based roasting or braising pan large enough to fit the lamb with some room around it, heat the 2 tablespoons of oil over medium-high heat. Transfer the lamb to a platter, reserving the marinade, and salt the lamb lightly all over. Sear the lamb on all sides until golden brown; this should take 12 to 15 minutes. Add enough broth to cover the bottom of the pan by about 1 inch. Add the tomatoes, shallots, and reserved marinade. Transfer the lamb to the oven and cook, basting it every 20 minutes or so and adding more broth as needed.

After 1¾ hours, add the potatoes and eggplant to the pan, tossing them with the tomatoes and pan juices. Continue cooking until the

½ cup plus 2 tablespoons extra virgin olive oil

3 fresh rosemary sprigs

6 to 8 garlic cloves

Pinch of crushed red pepper flakes

2 teaspoons kosher salt, plus more for salting the lamb

1 teaspoon freshly ground black pepper

1 whole leg of lamb (about 6 pounds), well trimmed

1 medium eggplant, cut into 1-inch cubes (about 2 cups)

4 to 6 cups Chicken Broth (page 241)

4 plum tomatoes, cut into sixths

1 cup quartered shallots

6 medium Yukon gold potatoes, cut into 1- to 1½-inch pieces

¼ cup chopped fresh basil

1 tablespoon chopped fresh parsley, plus more for garnish (optional)

lamb is fork-tender and the eggplant and potatoes are tender, too, about another 30 minutes.

TO FINISH   Transfer the lamb to a cutting board and let it rest for 15 minutes before carving. With a slotted spoon, retrieve the eggplant, potatoes, shallots, and any large pieces of tomato; keep the vegetables warm. Degrease the sauce left in the pan by skimming the clear fat from the surface using a large spoon or ladle. Heat the degreased sauce over medium-high heat to concentrate its flavors a bit.

Divide the vegetables among serving plates. Lay the lamb over the vegetables. Add the basil and parsley to the sauce and spoon the sauce over the lamb. Sprinkle with additional parsley, if you like, and serve immediately.

VENISON WITH RED WINE SAUCE WITH SEARED BACON AND SHALLOT DUMPLINGS SERVES 6 TO 8

This red wine sauce needs about one and a half hours of hands-off simmering time, but it's worth it. (Said my recipe tester after making it: "I want to marry this sauce.") While it's especially good when paired with full-flavored venison, you can substitute lamb or beef tenderloin if your market doesn't carry venison (or you don't have a hunter in your life). The rich, somewhat salty, smoky flavor of the dumplings goes exceptionally well with game. A few caramelized apple slices—sprinkle thinly sliced apple with sugar and cook over high heat until the slices are tender and well browned—or some Sautéed Broccoli Rabe (page 169) would also be welcome on the plate.

MAKE THE SAUCE IN ADVANCE   In a medium saucepan, heat 2 tablespoons of the olive oil over medium heat. Add the pancetta, shallots, cinnamon, and peppercorns and sauté, stirring occasionally, until the shallots are tender, about 7 minutes. Add the wine, honey, and apple. Reduce the heat to medium-low and cook the sauce until reduced by half, about 1 hour. Remove the pan from the heat and add the cassis, chicken reduction, and thyme. Return to the heat and continue cooking until the sauce has the consistency of thin oil, about another half hour. Strain through a fine mesh strainer. The sauce will keep for a week in the refrigerator and can also be frozen.

COOK THE VENISON   Heat the oven to 250°F. Season the meat all over with salt and pepper. Heat the remaining 2 tablespoons of olive oil in an ovenproof sauté pan and sear the venison on all sides until nicely browned, about 5 minutes. Transfer the pan to the oven to finish cooking to medium rare (135°F to 140°F), 30 to 50 minutes, depending on thickness and whether it's venison, lamb, or beef.

TO SERVE   Put one or two Seared Bacon and Shallot Dumplings on each warm serving plate. Slice the venison into ¼-inch-thick slices and fan them on the plate, partially covering the dumplings. Drizzle the red wine sauce over the venison and serve.

¼ cup olive oil

2 ounces pancetta, diced

3 small shallots, thinly sliced

¼ cinnamon stick or a pinch of ground cinnamon

1 scant teaspoon whole black peppercorns

2 cups deeply flavored, fruity red wine (I like a Lagrein from Alto Adige)

1 tablespoon honey

1 apple, peeled, cored, and diced

3 tablespoons crème de cassis

2 cups Chicken Reduction (page 242) or good-quality chicken base, reconstituted as the package directs until a little thicker than chicken broth

2 fresh thyme sprigs

2 pounds venison tenderloin (or 3 pounds lamb or beef tenderloin)

Kosher salt and freshly ground black pepper

Seared Bacon and Shallot Dumplings (recipe follows)

SEARED BACON AND SHALLOT DUMPLINGS

SERVES 6

Much of what I cook begins with a traditional Italian dish, in this case *gnocchi alla Romana,* a style of gnocchi that texturally has more in common with fried polenta than gnocchi made with potatoes. To go with deeply flavored game, I add bacon, shallots, and thyme to the semolina batter. The seared dumplings are delicious with venison; you can also serve them with a salad as a light lunch.

1 cup semolina flour

2 quarts whole milk

1 teaspoon kosher salt

Extra virgin olive oil as needed

2 medium shallots, finely chopped

4 slices bacon, finely diced

1 teaspoon chopped fresh thyme

$^1\!/_2$ cup all-purpose flour

4 large egg yolks, slightly beaten

MAKE THE SEMOLINA BATTER   In a medium saucepan over medium-high heat, whisk together the semolina, milk, and salt. Reduce the heat to low and cook, stirring occasionally, until quite thick, about 45 minutes.

Meanwhile, oil a quarter sheet pan or 9 by 13-inch baking pan, line it with parchment paper, and then oil the paper.

Heat 1 teaspoon of olive oil in a medium sauté pan over medium-high heat. Add the shallots, bacon, and thyme and cook until the bacon is crispy, adjusting the heat as needed. Reserve off the heat.

Add the all-purpose flour to the semolina batter, mixing it in well. Add the bacon and shallots and let cool to almost room temperature before beating in the egg yolks. Pour this mixture into the prepared pan and chill until quite firm, at least 4 hours and up to a day.

TO FINISH   Line a baking sheet with parchment paper. Heat the oven to 300°F. Using a 2-inch cookie cutter, stamp out 12 rounds of gnocchi (or use a knife to cut out similar size rectangles). Pour olive oil in a large nonstick sauté pan to a depth of ¼ inch and heat over medium-high heat. In batches if necessary, brown both sides of the gnocchi in the hot oil and transfer to the baking sheet. Finish heating the gnocchi through in the oven for 5 to 10 minutes.

Sweets, Cheese, and Breads

Most chefs are loath to admit it, but for most of us, desserts are our culinary Achilles heel. Though I know my way around pastry (thanks to a stint in Munich where I learned from a meticulous German master), it's just not what I do on a daily basis. I may know what I want a dessert to be, but I look to my pastry chefs to get it there. Fortunately, I worked with some fantastic, innovative people creating desserts that equal (they might say rival) the courses that have come before. What follows are some of their more accessible dessert recipes (and a couple of bread recipes, too).

I, myself, usually prefer to end a meal with a few excellent cheeses. A cheese course—I recommend serving at least three different cheeses—is especially good when entertaining at home where dinner guests often turn down dessert. Many decline because they're on diets or they're too full, but I find the main reason is that when you're entertaining at home, dessert, especially when served with coffee, signals the end of the evening. If the conversation around the table is a good one, people want to linger and have another glass of wine. This is the time for cheese.

What I like to do, especially if there is no actual dessert to come, is pair a bite of cheese with a little something sweet, whether a simple drizzle of aged balsamic vinegar over Parmigiano-Reggiano, a dab of honey and a grind of black pepper on some Gorgonzola dolce, or a spoonful of poached figs (page 233) with aged goat cheese. When carefully considered, the condiment draws out the essence of the cheese, highlighting what makes it unique. And because the servings are sized for just a bite or two, they leave diners satiated but not stuffed; you can keep pouring the wine from dinner or—even better—open up a bottle of late-harvest Riesling or Muscat.

ROASTED WHOLE PEARS WITH HAZELNUT, APRICOT, AND CRANBERRY STUFFING SERVES 6

For eating out of hand, nothing beats a soft, juicy pear—one whose flesh yields easily when pressed on (or bitten into). For this warm and toasty dessert, however, you want to start with firm ripe pears, which can be cored without bruising and will keep their shape during roasting. You'll know a pear is ripe enough if it gives just a little when pressed near the stem. Never bake with rock-hard, underripe pears—all the baking in the world will not help those. Better to wait a few days for them to ripen on the counter and choose another dessert in the meantime. You can use just about any variety of pear you like—Anjou, Bosc, or Bartlett. If you want to use tiny Seckels, which look adorable on the plate, serve two or three per person.

$^1/_2$ cup honey, preferably rosemary honey

$^1/_4$ cup chopped dried apricots

$^1/_4$ cup chopped dried cranberries

$^3/_4$ cup toasted chopped hazelnuts

6 pears, just barely ripe

Vanilla or Honey Gelato (page 218) or your own favorite ice cream

PLUMP THE FRUIT   Combine the ½ cup of honey with ½ cup water in a small saucepan. Bring to a boil, add the apricots and cranberries, and take off the heat. Allow the fruit to soften for 10 minutes. Strain the fruit over a bowl to capture the soaking liquid and reserve.

GRIND THE HAZELNUTS   Reserve ¼ cup of the hazelnuts. Grind the rest finely in a small food processor.

PEEL AND CORE THE PEARS   Leaving any stems on the pears, peel them carefully, following the contours of the fruit. To core and hollow out the pears, start from the bottom and cut out a small amount of the bottom of the pear with a paring knife, then continue digging upward, scooping out the flesh with a melon baller (or the tip of the paring knife) until all of the core is removed and you have made a cavity that will hold a couple of tablespoons of the filling.

STUFF AND BAKE THE PEARS   Line a sheet pan with parchment and heat the oven to 350°F. Combine the fruit with the ground hazelnuts and stuff the filling inside the pear. Stand the pears upright on the pan and brush all over with the reserved soaking liquid. Roast the pears, basting every 5 minutes or so, until tender and heated throughout, 20 to 25 minutes.

TO SERVE   Place a pear and a spoonful of ice cream on each plate and garnish with the reserved hazelnuts. Serve the pears while still warm.

NUTELLA PANINI WITH ICE CREAM AND ESPRESSO SERVES 2

Nutella is a brand of hazelnut and chocolate spread famous throughout Italy and the world. I love the stuff. Also known as gianduja, the nut and chocolate combination goes especially well with the hint of coffee added by a sprinkling of ground espresso beans. This dessert is incredibly quick and simple—if you can make a peanut butter sandwich you can make this—yet deliciously satisfying. This recipe makes two panini, but of course you can multiply it as you like.

MAKE THE PANINI   Heat a panini or sandwich grill until hot (about 400°F). If you don't have a panini grill, heat a grill pan or cast-iron pan over medium-high heat. Make two Nutella sandwiches. Brush the outsides of the bread with the melted butter. Grill in the press for 5 minutes. If using a pan, weight the sandwiches with foil-wrapped bricks or another heavy pan set on top.

TO SERVE   Cut each sandwich in half on the diagonal. Lay one half flat on the plate and lean the other half against the flat one for a little height. Top each sandwich with a dollop of ice cream and a sprinkle of ground espresso. Serve immediately.

Four ¹/₂-inch slices brioche

¹/₄ cup Nutella

1¹/₂ tablespoons melted butter

Vanilla Gelato (page 218) or your own favorite vanilla ice cream

2 pinches ground espresso beans

INDIVIDUAL CREAMY CHEESE TARTS WITH STRAWBERRIES AND BALSAMIC VINEGAR SERVES 8 TO 10

This free-form tart, made with a simple cookie base, is reminiscent of cheesecake but with a much lighter feel. The hard-cooked egg in the cookie dough adds a wonderful richness, but you can leave it out. For a very big party, this recipe is easily doubled.

FOR THE FILLING

$1/4$ cup whole milk

$1/2$ teaspoon Knox brand powdered gelatin (see Note)

$1/4$ cup plus 2 tablespoons heavy cream

$1/4$ cup sugar

1 egg yolk

$1/2$ cup plus 2 tablespoons fromage blanc or cream cheese

$1/2$ teaspoon vanilla extract (optional)

FOR THE COOKIES

$3/4$ cup all-purpose flour, plus more for rolling the dough

$1^1/2$ tablespoons unsweetened cocoa powder

$1/2$ teaspoon baking powder

$1/4$ teaspoon table salt

$6^1/2$ tablespoons unsalted butter, softened

$2^1/2$ tablespoons confectioners' sugar

$1/2$ hard-boiled egg pressed through a fine mesh strainer (optional)

MAKE THE FILLING   Pour 2 tablespoons of the milk into a tiny bowl. Soften the powdered gelatin by sprinkling it evenly over the milk. Let stand for a few minutes to soften. Meanwhile, combine the rest of the milk with the cream and sugar in a small saucepan and bring to a boil.

Whisk the egg yolk in a small bowl. Take the cream off the heat and whisk a tablespoon of it into the egg yolk to temper it. Add additional hot cream, a tablespoon or two at a time, until you have added about half of it. Pour the cream and egg back into the saucepan. Add the milk with the gelatin to the hot cream mixture and stir well to combine. Strain into a clean bowl, let cool a little, and stir in the fromage blanc along with the vanilla, if using. Refrigerate until totally congealed. (You can make the filling to this point a day or two ahead.)

MAKE THE CRUST   Combine the flour, cocoa, baking powder, and salt in a bowl. In a stand mixer with the paddle attachment, cream the butter and confectioners' sugar. Add the dry ingredients in batches until incorporated, then fold in the hard-boiled egg, if using.

Heat the oven to 350°F and line a baking sheet with parchment paper or a Silpat liner. Roll the dough on a lightly floured surface about ¼ inch thick and punch out 10 circles with a 2½-inch round cutter. Bake until the center of the cookie feels firm and the edges are just starting to turn a shade darker, about 10 minutes. Once cooled, the cookies will keep in an airtight container for 2 to 3 days.

TO FINISH   Spoon the cold filling into the bowl of a stand mixer fitted with a whisk and beat until the mixture lightens considerably and increases in volume.

Combine the strawberries, mint, orange zest, and balsamic vinegar. Season to taste with a little sugar.

Put the cookies on serving plates. Divide the filling among the cookies, either spooning it on or piping it on with a pastry bag. Top with the strawberries and serve.

NOTE   Pastry chefs prefer using sheet gelatin; if you want to use that in place of the powdered gelatin, soften one sheet in cold water for 10 minutes. Squeeze the sheet dry and add it to the hot cream and milk mixture.

FOR THE TOPPING

2 pints strawberries, sliced

3 fresh mint leaves, cut into a chiffonade

$1/4$ teaspoon finely grated orange zest

2 tablespoons good-quality balsamic vinegar

Sugar

PUFF PASTRY APRICOT "TATIN" WITH THYME ZABAGLIONE SERVES 8

To quote my recipe tester, "This tart is very, very easy to make." Because you use frozen puff pastry and purchased apricot jam, the "tatin" comes together quickly. You can have the elements prepared—the pastry circle cut, the apricots pitted—and then bake it just before serving, as it's best still warm from the oven. Though the pastry would be delicious with the ice cream or the zabaglione alone, the warm and cold contrast of the two accompaniments is just wonderful. If you have a stand mixer, you can make the zabaglione as much as two hours ahead, though you do need to keep whisking it at the lowest speed the entire time. I like the rustic look of halved apricots, but you can slice the apricots, if you'd rather.

4 small fresh thyme sprigs

1/4 cup plus 2 tablespoons sugar

1 sheet good-quality frozen puff pastry, slightly thawed

2 tablespoons apricot jam, plus more if needed

1 pound apricots (about 6), cut in half through the stem, pit removed

4 large egg yolks

Honey Gelato (page 218) or your own favorite vanilla ice cream

MAKE A SIMPLE SYRUP   In a small saucepan, combine the thyme, the 1/4 cup sugar, and 1/4 cup water. Bring to a boil and cook just until the sugar dissolves. Remove from heat and allow the thyme to steep for an hour. Strain into a clean container. If not using right away, store in the refrigerator; this simple syrup will keep for weeks.

MAKE THE TATIN   Position one of the oven racks to the lower middle of the oven and heat the oven to 375°F. Line a baking sheet with a Silpat or parchment paper.

Lightly roll out one sheet of puff pastry to increase its size just a bit to 10 inches. Cut the sheet into a 10-inch circle. (Return the circle to the freezer if not using immediately.) Put the puff pastry on the prepared baking sheet and brush it with the apricot jam, leaving a border of about 1½ inches. Put the apricots, cut side down, on the puff pastry, arranging them in a ring on top of the jam. Sprinkle the apricots well with the 2 tablespoons of sugar and bake until the pastry browns and the apricots begin to caramelize, 15 to 25 minutes (begin checking on the early side). For more caramelization, briefly run the pastry under the broiler. *(continued)*

MAKE THE ZABAGLIONE   Combine the simple syrup with the egg yolks in a metal bowl that you can set over a saucepan of boiling water to make a double boiler. (If you plan to use a stand mixer for whisking—a good idea—use the mixer's own bowl.) Whisk by hand until frothy, then put the bowl over the simmering water and cook, whisking constantly and adjusting the heat as necessary, until the yolks are cooked to the ribbon stage. This means they lighten in color and thicken, and when the whisk is lifted, the dripping yolks form a ribbonlike pattern before sinking back into the mixture a few seconds later. At this point, take the bowl off the heat and, if using a stand mixer, put it on the stand. Whisk continuously at high speed until the mixture cools to room temperature and the texture is like a very lightly whipped cream. If not serving immediately, continue to whisk the zabaglione on very low speed to prevent it from separating.

TO SERVE   Cut the tart into slices. Position a small scoop of ice cream and a spoonful of the zabaglione alongside the slice and serve immediately.

ROCHER (CRISPY CHOCOLATE BITES) MAKES 20 TO 30 PIECES

I like to serve these little bites of chocolate on a plate with dainty cookies and truffles. Although all of the sweets are delicious, I can tell diners find these the most fun to eat. *Feuilletine* are thin, crisp wheat flakes. You can find them at specialty cooking stores or through mail order. But you can also go the more pedestrian route and substitute good old cornflakes—just break the flakes up a little first. Once you get the idea of how to make these candies, you can also experiment with using puffed rice cereal or even soy nuts to give the chocolates their crunch. These will keep for a week refrigerated and for just about forever if frozen.

Line a sheet pan with parchment paper. Melt all the chocolate in a double boiler or in the microwave. Add the salt and stir. Add the *feuilletine* and mix well. Using a couple of demitasse or similar-size spoons, collect a heaping spoonful of the chocolate-covered flakes and use another spoon to push the clump onto the prepared sheet. Chill the candies until quite firm, then serve or freeze.

7 ounces bittersweet (65%) chocolate, chopped

7 ounces milk chocolate, chopped

Pinch of kosher salt

2 cups *feuilletine* or lightly crumbled cornflakes (you want $^1/_4$- to $^1/_3$-inch pieces)

GELATO (ICE CREAM) MAKES ABOUT 1 QUART

Essentially Italian ice cream, gelato traditionally uses less cream and more milk than most typical American ice cream, and is thus generally lower in fat. However, it still has a dense texture and a rich mouthfeel, thanks in large part to the addition of dry milk powder. That ingredient and the yolks add fat to the gelato but not the butterfat that a lot of cream contributes, which can feel almost greasy in your mouth. Consider this recipe a base to play with, and then tweak the added ingredients (those listed here or lifted from your own imagination) to get exactly the flavor you want. (After all, that is the true joy of making your own ice cream, isn't it?) Finally, you can fold in any harder additions—toasted nuts, raisins, finely chopped Peanut Brittle (page 222), or bits of chocolate—before the ice cream is completely frozen.

5 large egg yolks

2 1/4 cups whole milk

1/3 cup heavy cream

1/2 cup sugar

1 tablespoon light corn syrup

1/4 cup nonfat dry milk

Whisk the egg yolks in a medium bowl. In a large, heavy-based saucepan, combine the milk, cream, sugar, corn syrup, and dry milk. Bring just to a boil over high heat. Remove from heat and stir a few tablespoons of the hot milk mixture into the eggs, whisking constantly. Continue adding more of the milk mixture, a little bit at a time and stirring, until you have added about half of it. (This step prevents the eggs from being scrambled by the addition of the hot liquid all at once.) Add the rest of the milk mixture, stir to combine, and strain through a fine mesh strainer into a clean bowl.

Fill a larger bowl with ice and set the bowl with the gelato mixture on the ice to cool it rapidly. Stir occasionally to speed the cooling. Freeze according to your ice cream maker's directions.

CARAMEL   Start with just the sugar and corn syrup in the pan; cook it until it turns golden brown. Carefully add the remaining ingredients (the caramel will sputter) and bring to a boil while stirring.

CARDAMOM   Add 10 whole cardamom pods to the milk-cream mixture before heating.

CHOCOLATE   Add 4 ounces of your favorite chocolate (chopped) to the hot ice cream base as you are tempering the eggs.

COFFEE   Add 2 tablespoons ground espresso beans to the milk-cream mixture before heating.

HONEY   Replace the sugar and corn syrup with the same amount of honey.

MINT   Add a large handful of mint leaves to the milk-cream mixture before heating.

MUSCOVADO   Replace all of the sugar and corn syrup with muscovado sugar.

SAFFRON   Crumble 2 teaspoons saffron threads into the milk-cream mixture before heating.

VANILLA   Split 3 vanilla beans and scrape the insides into the milk-cream mixture (you can throw the pods in, too) before heating. Or, add 2 teaspoons good-quality vanilla extract after chilling the ice cream mixture.

TIM'S CHOCOLATE CAKE WITH PEANUT BRITTLE AND BITTERSWEET CHOCOLATE SAUCE SERVES 12 TO 16, DEPENDING ON SIZE OF MOLDS

This is one very forgiving dessert. Bake the cake a little under, and the center is marvelously molten; bake it a little longer and the middle firms more but is delicious and moist nonetheless. The peanut brittle makes the dessert more whimsical in its presentation, and its saltiness also complements and enhances the deep flavor of the not-too-sweet cake.

1/2 pound good-quality bittersweet chocolate, such as Valrhona, coarsely chopped

1/2 pound unsalted butter (2 sticks), cut into chunks

2 large eggs

8 large egg yolks

6 tablespoons sugar

3 tablespoons plus 1 teaspoon all-purpose flour

Nonstick cooking spray

Bittersweet Chocolate Sauce (recipe follows)

Peanut Brittle (recipe follows)

Vanilla Gelato (page 218) or your own favorite vanilla ice cream (optional)

MAKE THE BATTER   In a double boiler, melt the chocolate and butter together, stirring occasionally. Keep a close eye on the heat to avoid scorching the chocolate. Let the mixture cool briefly before whisking in the whole eggs and egg yolks. Sift the sugar and flour into the chocolate. (You can prepare the batter well in advance of baking the cakes; simply cover tightly and refrigerate for up to a week.)

PREPARE YOUR CAKE MOLDS   Heat the oven to 350°F. Bottomless 3-inch round metal rings set on a heavy-bottomed sheet pan work well. Individual tart pans and ramekins should work, too. You can even make one larger cake, though you will need to increase the baking time. Whichever mold you use, spray it (as well as the baking sheet, if using bottomless molds) with nonstick cooking spray.

BAKE THE CAKES   Divide the batter among the molds, leaving at least the top 1/2 inch of the mold empty. Bake until the edges just begin to look dry, 4 to 5 minutes for a 3-inch mold. The center will still be slightly liquid but will firm up a little more from the residual heat. Let cool on the baking sheet before unmolding the cakes. To loosen them, run a knife around the side of the mold.

TO SERVE   Smear a little of the chocolate sauce on each dessert plate. Place a cake on the sauce. Top the cake with more sauce and serve with a shard of the peanut brittle and some ice cream, if you like.

PEANUT BRITTLE

MAKES A HALF SHEET PAN OF BRITTLE

Unlike traditional peanut brittle, which suspends whole peanuts in a caramel, this brittle is made from ground peanuts, which makes the shards smooth and glasslike. Combining the ground peanuts with the caramel and reheating them together gently protects the peanuts from scorching, as they might if put directly into the liquid caramel.

Nonstick cooking spray

2 cups sugar

5 tablespoons unsalted butter, cut into chunks

2 cups (about 11 ounces) salted, dry-roasted peanuts, ground in a food processor

MAKE THE CARAMEL   Line a half sheet pan or similar size (13 by 18 inches) sided baking sheet with a Silpat or parchment paper. Spray with nonstick cooking spray.

In a heavy-based saucepan, caramelize the sugar by heating it until liquid and golden brown. Take the pan off the heat and stir in the butter, being careful as the caramel will sputter. Quickly pour the caramel onto the prepared baking sheet and spread it by quickly and carefully tilting the pan to get it to flow into a thin layer. As it cools, use a heatproof spatula to spread it evenly. Let cool completely.

TO FINISH   Heat the oven to 350°F. Break the cooled and hardened caramel into pieces and grind them finely in a food processor. As before, line a half sheet pan with a Silpat or parchment and spray with nonstick cooking spray. Combine the ground caramel and ground peanuts. Spread the grinds in a thin but cohesive layer on the prepared pan. Bake until golden brown, about 12 minutes. Let cool completely before cracking the brittle into shards. Store the cooled brittle in an airtight container for up to a week.

BITTERSWEET CHOCOLATE SAUCE
MAKES ABOUT 2 CUPS

This classic, all-purpose sauce is exceedingly easy to make. Store it in the fridge and reheat as needed.

1 cup heavy cream
$1/2$ pound good-quality bittersweet chocolate, such as Valrhona

In a heavy-based saucepan, heat the cream until boiling. Remove the pan from the heat, add the chocolate, and let it sit for a minute before stirring.

CAMPARI CITRUS SALAD WITH ORANGE CUSTARD "FRENCH TOAST" SERVES 6

This is one sexy dessert. I like a mix of citrus, for both looks and flavor. If blood oranges are not in season, however, simply add another sweet orange to the mix. We serve this with tarragon ice cream, which you can make at home by adding pureed tarragon to the ice cream base on page 218. Or, even easier, add a little fresh tarragon to the salad and top it with your favorite vanilla, chocolate, or ginger ice cream. Finally, I like to add just a few drops of good-quality extra virgin olive oil to the plate for a grassy, spicy finish that goes especially well with the fruit.

FOR THE CITRUS SALAD

1 orange

1 lemon (a Meyer lemon would be especially nice)

1 tangerine

1 blood orange

1 grapefruit

1 cup sugar

1 shot Campari

$1/2$ vanilla bean, split, or $1/2$ teaspoon vanilla extract

1 teaspoon finely chopped fresh tarragon

SEGMENT THE FRUIT For each fruit, cut off both ends. Using a sharp, flexible knife and a sawing motion, cut away the skin and white membrane from top to bottom, following the contours of the fruit. Free the segments by cutting along the seams that separate one segment from the other. Combine all of the segments in a heatproof bowl.

MAKE A SIMPLE SYRUP Combine the sugar, 1 cup water, the Campari, and the vanilla in a saucepan and bring to a boil over medium-high heat. Reduce to a simmer and continue to cook until the sugar has dissolved. Pour the hot liquid over the fruit. Let it come to room temperature (stirring the bowl over ice makes this happen more quickly) before chilling well in the refrigerator. Once cooled, stir in the tarragon (omit if serving with tarragon ice cream, however).

MAKE THE CUSTARD Whisk the egg yolks and sugar together in a medium bowl. Combine the milk, cream, and orange zest in a medium saucepan and bring just to a boil over high heat. Turn off the heat and let the orange infuse the liquid for a few minutes. Gradually stir a few tablespoons of the hot cream mixture into the eggs, whisking constantly. Continue adding a bit more until you have stirred in about half of the mixture. Return the egg and cream mixture to the saucepan and stir to combine. Strain through a fine mesh strainer into a high-sided baking pan to soak the bread easily. (You can make the custard ahead and cool it until ready to make the "French toast.")

MAKE THE "FRENCH TOAST"   Heat the oven to 250°F. Line a baking sheet, cutting board, or platter with paper towels. Soak the bread slices in the custard until thoroughly soaked, a minute or two, turning if need be. Transfer to the paper towels. Melt 2 tablespoons butter in a large sauté pan or griddle over medium heat. When quite hot, cook the bread in batches until well browned on each side, 3 to 4 minutes per side, adding more butter if needed. Keep the cooked slices warm in the oven while you make the rest.

TO SERVE   Put two slices of the "French toast" on each serving dish. Top with a rounded spoonful of ice cream. Use a slotted spoon to remove the citrus slices from the sauce and top the ice cream with some of the fruit. Drizzle some of the sauce over the fruit and around the plate, add a few drops of olive oil if using, and serve immediately.

FOR THE "FRENCH TOAST"

$2/3$ cup egg yolks (about 8 large)

$2/3$ cup sugar

1 cup whole milk

1 cup heavy cream

Zest from 1 orange

12 thick (about 1-inch) slices fine-grained bread, preferably brioche

2 to 3 tablespoons unsalted butter, plus more if needed

Vanilla, chocolate, or mint ice cream

Few drops of extra virgin olive oil (optional)

TIRAMISU PARFAIT SERVES 8

Serve this coffee-flavored dessert in clear parfait glasses or large martini glasses with a spoon. Though these are best when made with the Espresso Ladyfingers, you *could* cheat and layer the mousse with purchased ladyfingers. Whichever kind you use, give the ladyfingers just a brief dip in the coffee-flavored syrup; allow the outside to soften but leave the middle still firm. Otherwise the ladyfingers may fall apart as you transfer them from syrup to serving dish.

5 sheets gelatin or 2$\frac{1}{2}$ teaspoons Knox brand unflavored powdered gelatin

$\frac{1}{3}$ cup plus 1 tablespoon coffee liqueur

4 large egg whites

6 large egg yolks

$\frac{2}{3}$ cup plus $\frac{1}{2}$ cup sugar

Pinch of kosher salt

1 teaspoon vanilla extract (optional)

8 ounces mascarpone

$\frac{1}{3}$ cup heavy cream, whipped to medium-firm peaks

2 tablespoons espresso or very strong coffee

Espresso Ladyfingers (recipe follows)

Chocolate shavings

SOFTEN THE GELATIN   If using sheet gelatin, soften the sheets in cold water for 10 minutes before using. If using powdered gelatin, pour it on top of the $\frac{1}{3}$ cup coffee liqueur in a small bowl.

WHISK THE EGGS   In a stand mixer with the whisk attachment, whisk the egg whites on medium speed until very soft peaks appear. Add $\frac{1}{3}$ cup of the sugar and continue beating until the whites are glossy with medium-stiff peaks. In a separate bowl, whisk together the egg yolks, $\frac{1}{3}$ cup of the sugar, the salt, and the vanilla, if using, to the ribbon stage. (See the description on page 216.)

MAKE THE MOUSSE   Put the mascarpone in a large mixing bowl. Put the $\frac{1}{3}$ cup of coffee liqueur (which will include the gelatin, if using the powdered type) in a small saucepan. If using the gelatin sheets, remove them from the water and squeeze them dry before adding them to the coffee liqueur. Stir over medium heat to melt the gelatin. Pour this hot liquid over the mascarpone and mix well. Mix in the egg yolks, then fold in the egg whites. Finally, fold in the whipped cream.

ASSEMBLE AND SERVE   Divide *half* of the mousse among serving bowls or glasses and refrigerate these as well as the remaining mousse.

Combine the $\frac{1}{2}$ cup of sugar with $\frac{1}{2}$ cup of water and bring to a boil.

Reduce to a simmer and cook just until the sugar dissolves. Let cool a bit, then add the 1 tablespoon of coffee liqueur and the espresso. When the syrup is just warm or at room temperature, submerge the ladyfingers in it briefly, letting each soak for a few seconds. Add a layer of ladyfingers to each parfait glass, 2 or 3 per serving, depending on the size of the bowl or glass. Spoon the reserved mousse over the ladyfingers. If not serving right away, cover the parfaits with plastic wrap and refrigerate. (You can assemble them up to 8 hours ahead.) Just before serving, garnish with some chocolate curls or shavings.

ESPRESSO LADYFINGERS

MAKES ABOUT 30 LADYFINGERS

The espresso in these ladyfingers makes them truly irresistible. You may have a few more than you need, depending on the size of your serving glasses, which is fine since they make a nice snack—with a cup of espresso, of course. Once cooled, you can wrap the ladyfingers well in plastic and keep them at room temperature for a day or freeze them for longer storage.

3 large egg whites

$^2/_3$ cup sugar

5 large egg yolks

2 tablespoons instant espresso (dried, not prepared)

$^3/_4$ cup all-purpose flour

Nonstick cooking spray

WHISK THE EGGS   In a stand mixer with the whisk attachment, whisk the egg whites on medium speed until very soft peaks appear. Add ⅓ cup of the sugar and continue beating until the whites are glossy with medium-stiff peaks. In a separate bowl, whisk the yolks with the remaining ⅓ cup of sugar and the instant espresso to the ribbon stage (see page 216). With a large flexible spatula, gently fold half of the egg whites into the yolk mixture. Add the remaining whites and the flour and fold just until there are no more large streaks of egg white and the flour is well mixed.

SHAPE AND BAKE THE LADYFINGERS   Heat the oven to 350°F. Line a half sheet pan with a Silpat or parchment paper and spray with nonstick cooking spray.

Gently scoop the batter into a pastry bag. Pipe the batter onto the baking sheet in strips about 3 inches long and 1 inch wide, leaving about 1 inch between each ladyfinger. For best results, let the batter fall lightly from the bag and finish each ladyfinger with a quick lift of the wrist. Bake until springy to the touch, 14 to 16 minutes. Set on a rack and let cool to room temperature before using.

CHOCOLATE BISCOTTI   MAKES ABOUT 32 BISCOTTI

A dream biscotti for chocolate lovers. With the addition of pistachios and hazelnuts and their crisp exterior, these treats are more sophisticated than brownies (a little anyway), but they satisfy the same sweet craving.

Heat the oven to 325°F.

MAKE THE BATTER   In a large bowl, cream the butter and sugar by hand or using the paddle attachment on a stand mixer. Add the honey, eggs, and vanilla and almond extracts and beat until fluffy. In a separate bowl, combine the flour, cocoa, baking powder, and salt. Add this to the butter-sugar mixture in a few additions. Finally, mix in the hazelnuts, pistachios, and chocolate chips.

SHAPE THE DOUGH AND BAKE ONCE   On a piece of parchment paper or foil about the size of your baking sheet, shape the batter into a log about 16 inches long, 4 inches wide, and 1 inch high (this does not have to be exact and you can vary the width depending on what length you want the final biscotti to be). Slide the whole thing onto the baking sheet. Brush the top with some beaten egg white and sprinkle lightly with sugar. Bake the log until it feels pretty firm to the touch, about 50 minutes; the log will spread somewhat. Set the sheet on a rack until the log is cool enough to handle, about 30 minutes.

SLICE THE BISCOTTI AND BAKE AGAIN   Line two baking sheets with parchment paper. Reduce the oven temperature to 225°F. Slice the log crosswise into pieces about ½ inch thick. Return the slices to the baking sheets, laying them flat, and bake until the edges begin to become dry and crispy, another 25 to 30 minutes. They will not feel completely crisp until cooled, however. Once completely cooled, store in an airtight container.

10 tablespoons unsalted butter, at room temperature

1 cup sugar, plus more for sprinkling

$1/4$ cup honey

2 large eggs

$1 1/2$ teaspoons vanilla extract

$1 1/2$ teaspoons almond extract

3 cups all-purpose flour

$1/2$ cup cocoa powder (not Dutch process)

2 teaspoons baking powder

$1/2$ teaspoon salt

$1/2$ cup skinned whole hazelnuts

$1/2$ cup shelled pistachios

$1/2$ cup chocolate chips

1 large egg white, lightly beaten

MUSCOVADO CAKE WITH CARAMEL APPLE SAUCE SERVES 6

If you can't find muscovado sugar, use dark brown sugar. This makes more cake than you will need to serve six; freeze any leftover cake, well wrapped in plastic, for up to three months to serve another time.

Nonstick cooking spray

$^3/_4$ cup egg whites (about 7 large)

$1^1/_2$ cups muscovado sugar

$^3/_4$ cup egg yolks (about 11 large)

1 cup plus 3 tablespoons all-purpose flour

1 cup granulated sugar

2 tablespoons brandy or apple cider

2 tablespoons unsalted butter

12 small lady apples, peeled, cored, and halved, or 8 medium apples of your choice, peeled, cored, and sliced into eighths

Muscovado Gelato (page 218) or vanilla ice cream

$^1/_4$ cup toasted sliced almonds

BAKE THE CAKE   Line a half sheet pan with a Silpat or parchment paper and spray with nonstick cooking spray. Heat the oven to 350°F. In a stand mixer with the whisk attachment, whisk the egg whites on medium speed until very soft peaks appear. Add ½ cup of the muscovado sugar and continue beating until the whites are glossy with medium-stiff peaks. In a separate bowl, whisk the egg yolks with ½ cup of the muscavado sugar until tripled in volume. Sift the flour into the egg yolks and whisk briefly to combine. With a large flexible spatula, gently fold half of the egg whites into the yolk mixture. Add the remaining half of the whites and fold just until there are no more large streaks of white. Spread the batter on the prepared pan and bake until springy to the touch, 10 minutes. Transfer to a cooling rack. Once cool, cut 6 individual-size pieces from the cake (either 2-inch squares or 2-inch rounds). The rest can be frozen.

MAKE A SIMPLE SYRUP   In a small saucepan, combine the remaining ½ cup of muscovado sugar with ½ cup of water. Bring to a boil and cook just until the sugar dissolves. Cool to room temperature before using. (The simple syrup can be made ahead and kept refrigerated for a couple of weeks; it's also an excellent sweetener for iced tea and cocktails.)

MAKE THE CARAMEL APPLE SAUCE   In a large (14-inch is best), heavy-based sauté pan, heat the granulated sugar over high heat, swirling the pan by the handle but not stirring, until the sugar dissolves and turns light brown, about 5 minutes. Add the brandy—be aware that the alcohol may ignite but the flame will quickly go out— and the butter. Take the pan off the heat and carefully swirl it to incorporate the liquid and the butter. Add the apples to the pan and cook in the sauce over medium-high heat until they are just tender but still hold their shape, about 8 minutes; adjust the heat as needed to prevent the sugar from burning. The apples will release their juices into the caramel, making it a little less thick, which is good. (The apples can be cooked in advance and taste even better for it. Remove them from the sauce and store both the sauce and the apples until ready to use. Reheat them together over medium heat before serving.)

TO SERVE   Using a pastry brush, lightly brush the cake with the simple syrup. Top with a small scoop of gelato and some of the warm caramel apple sauce. Sprinkle with the almonds and serve immediately.

PRESENTING THE CHEESE COURSE

For the best cheese course, begin with the best cheeses. Supermarkets are getting better cheese selections, some even featuring artisanal cheeses, but you will still do better visiting a store that specializes in cheese. The people working there will likely be more knowledgeable and will handle the cheese with the care it deserves. (For most cheeses, especially soft ones, this precludes plastic wrap.) If no good cheese can be found within driving distance, consider mail-ordering cheese for a special occasion. Most of the cheeses I recommend here (and absolutely love) you can get from Murray's Cheese in New York City (see Sources), either in person or by mail.

When presenting cheese, make a show of it to let guests know this is more than your average cheese-and-cracker spread. Offer a composed tasting of different cheeses by plating individual portions of three (or more) cheeses, leaving plenty of room between them. I like to serve cheeses with a sweet condiment, positioning the cheese so it's half on and half off the condiment with just the tiniest bit of the condiment drizzled over the cheese. This not only looks pretty, but it also ensures the plate is mostly about the cheese, as it should be. For even more wow factor, present each cheese and its condiment on its own tiny plate and put a row of plates in front of each guest. For a much more casual presentation, present the cheese whole next to the condiment it's paired with and let guests help themselves.

After trying these condiments, you may want to experiment with creating your own sweet and cheese pairings, such as apple puree with pecorino or peaches and balsamic vinegar with fresh goat cheese, or a soft blue cheese with pears and almonds.

Finally, although the breads that end this chapter are served at the start of the meal at the restaurants, they would also be delicious served with cheese, most especially the Walnut-Currant Bread on page 238.

AGED GOAT CHEESE WITH CHAMOMILE-SCENTED FIGS
SERVES 6 TO 8 AS PART OF A CHEESE COURSE

Soaking dried figs in chamomile adds a subtle floral note to the figs' sweet richness.

POACH THE FIGS   In a small saucepan, bring 1 cup of water to a boil. Add the tea bags and sugar and let the tea steep for 3 or 4 minutes. Remove the tea bags. Add the figs and simmer gently until the figs are plump and tender, 10 to 12 minutes. Let cool and serve at room temperature or chilled.

TO SERVE   Serve the cheese with about 1 heaping teaspoon of the figs per serving.

2 chamomile tea bags

1/2 teaspoon sugar

6 dried figs, diced

6 to 8 ounces aged goat cheese, such as Boucheron

LA TUR WITH PINE NUT AND RAISIN *MOSTARDA*

SERVES 6 TO 8 AS PART OF A CHEESE COURSE

Made from a blend of goat, cow, and sheep milk, La Tur is both dense and creamy; it has an earthy flavor that really responds to the sweetness of the raisins and the tingly heat of the mustard oil. Other cheeses that I really like with this *mostarda* include Jasper Hill Farm Constant Bliss, which is made in Vermont, or a Castelrosso, which like La Tur hails from Piedmont. If your market doesn't carry mustard oil, look for it at Asian food markets and in health food stores.

1 cup golden raisins

2 tablespoons toasted chopped pine nuts

1 teaspoon chopped fresh lemon verbena (optional)

1 teaspoon mustard oil

6 to 8 ounces La Tur or similar cheese

STEEP THE FRUIT   Bring 1 cup of water to a boil in a small saucepan. Add the raisins, pine nuts, and lemon verbena, if using, and take the pan off the heat. Let steep for 5 to 6 minutes before adding the mustard oil. Cool to room temperature before serving.

TO SERVE   Serve the cheese with about 1 heaping tablespoon of the *mostarda* per serving.

RICOTTA WITH LEMON AND POPPY SEED MARMALADE

SERVES 6 TO 8 AS PART OF A CHEESE COURSE

Sweet, tart, and packing a little heat, this easy-to-make condiment complements mild cheeses without overwhelming. If you can't get buffalo-milk ricotta, pick the best quality sheep's milk or cow's milk ricotta you can find. I'm not talking about the watery stuff sold in plastic tubs; I'm talking about cheese that's sold by weight, wrapped in paper, and soft yet holding its shape. Look for fresh ricotta at a good cheese shop or Italian market. Ask for a taste before buying; fresh ricotta should taste mildly sweet and nutty; if sharp, it's likely past its prime.

PREPARE THE LEMONS   Leaving the skin on, cut the lemons into 1-inch dice. Toss the lemon with the sugar, then cover and marinate at least 8 hours and up to 24 hours.

MAKE THE MARMALADE   Dice the lemon a little smaller, then cook it in a small saucepan over medium heat until it forms a syrup consistency, about 15 minutes. (Add up to ¼ cup water if the lemons are not very juicy.) Stir in the poppy seeds and red pepper flakes and cool to room temperature.

TO SERVE   Serve the cheese with about 1 heaping teaspoon of the marmalade per serving.

2 whole lemons, scrubbed

½ cup sugar

1 tablespoon poppy seeds

Pinch of crushed red pepper flakes

6 to 8 ounces imported ricotta di bufala

SEMOLINA BREAD MAKES 3 MEDIUM LOAVES

Don't be afraid when you see the word *starter* in this recipe. It's easily made and proofs in an hour. Though directions are given for making the bread into boules, or round loaves, you could also shape the dough into baguettes or rolls. Delicious served warm, it makes fabulous sandwiches the next day.

FOR THE STARTER

2 cups (10 ounces) semolina flour

1/4 teaspoon active dry yeast

FOR THE DOUGH

4 cups (20 ounces) semolina flour

1 teaspoon active dry yeast

1 1/2 tablespoons kosher salt

All-purpose or semolina flour for dusting

MAKE THE STARTER   In a bowl, mix the semolina flour, yeast, and 1¾ cups water, adding up to ½ cup more water if needed. Set the bowl somewhere warm (75°F to 80°F) to proof for an hour. This mixture will look porridgy and not doughlike.

KNEAD THE DOUGH   Fit a stand mixer with the dough hook. Combine the semolina flour, yeast, and salt. Add the proofed starter and knead on medium speed until the dough is smooth, about 10 minutes. Let the dough rest for 5 minutes and then knead again for 5 minutes; the dough should be elastic and should clean itself off the sides of the bowl. Let the dough proof again for an hour and then punch it down.

SHAPE THE DOUGH   Sprinkle a baking sheet with flour. Divide the dough into three pieces with a pastry scraper. For each piece, tuck the dough into itself to stretch the outer skin of one side; continue tucking until one side of the dough looks like a tight, round ball; the other will look bunched. Turn the dough so the bunched side is down on the work surface. The smooth side of the dough can be lightly floured so it doesn't stick to your hands, but your work surface should be relatively free of flour so that the bottom of the dough sticks ever so slightly (the friction against the table will build surface tension on the boule). Using both hands slightly cupped, rotate the bottom of the boule against the work surface, going round and round quite vigorously. As you do this, use the pinky side of your hands to tighten the top skin of the loaf and seal the bottom.

Put the boules on the prepared baking sheet with some room between them, dust them with a little flour, cover with plastic wrap, and let proof in a warm spot (75°F to 80°F) for 45 minutes. The loaves will puff up only about 10 percent in size.

BAKE THE BREAD   Heat the oven to 350°F. Humidify the oven by putting a dozen ice cubes in an ovenproof dish and setting the dish on the oven floor or a low rack below the bread. Score a cross in the top of each loaf using a straight-edge razor. Bake until golden brown, 25 to 30 minutes. Let cool until just warm before slicing. This bread is best served on its own the day it was made (preferably while still warm), but it makes really good sandwiches when a day old.

WALNUT-CURRANT BREAD MAKES 3 MEDIUM BAGUETTES OR BOULES

Fresh yeast works faster and longer than active dry yeast, but it's very perishable and loses potency a few weeks after it's packed. Pastry chefs, who use a lot of yeast, prefer it and buy big blocks of it. Most supermarkets that carry fresh yeast sell it as foil-wrapped cakes weighing 0.6 ounce or 2 ounces. Be sure to check the expiration date on yeast, especially fresh yeast, and don't use it if it's expired.

FOR THE "STARTER"

1/2 cup (2 1/2) ounces bread flour

1/3 cup (1 3/4) ounces whole wheat flour

FOR THE DOUGH

1/4 ounce fresh yeast (about half of a 0.6-ounce cube) or 1 1/4 teaspoons (about 1/2 packet) active dry yeast

1 1/2 teaspoons honey

1 tablespoon extra virgin olive oil

3 1/3 cups (16 ounces) bread flour

3/4 cup (3 1/2 ounces) whole wheat flour

1 1/2 tablespoons kosher salt

2 1/4 teaspoons sugar

1/3 cup miller's bran

1/3 cup whole milk

4 ounces walnut pieces, toasted and roughly chopped (about 3/4 cup)

4 ounces currants (about 2/3 cup)

Nonstick cooking spray

All-purpose or semolina flour for dusting

MAKE THE "STARTER" In a small bowl, combine the bread flour and 1/2 cup water. In another small bowl, combine the whole wheat flour and 1/3 cup water.

MAKE THE DOUGH In the bowl of a stand mixer with a dough hook, combine the fresh yeast with 1/2 cup of warm water to soften it. If using active dry yeast, combine it with 1/2 cup of warm water as well as the honey and let stand for 5 minutes. Add the olive oil (and the honey if it's not in already) and mix to combine. Add the bread flour, whole wheat flour, salt, sugar, and bran. Add the milk and 1/2 cup water. Add the starter and mix with the dough hook to combine. If the dough is still dry, add more water a little at a time until the dough comes together in a cohesive mass. Increase the speed to medium and knead the dough for 10 minutes. Let the dough rest for 5 minutes, then knead again for 8 minutes. Mix in the walnuts and currants.

PROOF THE DOUGH Spray a large bowl with nonstick cooking spray and put the dough in it. Let the dough rise to almost twice its size in a warm place (75°F to 80°F), about 1 hour. Punch the dough and cut it into three pieces with a bench knife.

SHAPE THE DOUGH Heat the oven to 350°F. Lightly flour two baking sheets. Divide the dough into three pieces. Shape the dough into boules as described on page 236 or into baguettes. For baguettes, press a piece of dough into a flat rectangle. Fold down the top third of the rectangle, pressing down to seal the dough. Fold the dough down again, this time in half, and seal this seam. Repeat this pressing and folding once or twice to form a short log with a tight skin. Gently roll the log out under your hands to make a baguette with slightly tapered ends. Place the loaves on the prepared sheets and let proof again in a warm spot (75°F to 80°F) for 30 minutes.

BAKE THE BREAD   Humidify the oven by putting a dozen ice cubes in an ovenproof dish and setting the dish on the oven floor or a low rack below the bread. Score a cross in the top of each loaf using a straight-edge razor and bake for 30 minutes, until the bread is a dark golden brown. Let cool a bit before slicing.

Feel free to experiment with the additions to this bread, using different nuts or golden raisins or dried cranberries in place of the currants.

Basics

CHICKEN BROTH MAKES ABOUT 2½ QUARTS

This chicken broth is very easy to make and much better than anything you will find in the store. I don't season the broth until I'm using it; that way I can adjust the amount of salt to suit the recipe.

POACH THE CHICKEN   Put the chickens, carrot, celery, onion, and thyme in a very large (about 10-quart) stockpot. Add cold water to cover, about 4 quarts. Bring to a bubbling simmer over high heat, then lower the heat to maintain a gentle simmer for about 2 hours, until the flavor is extracted from the chickens. Every so often, skim the scum that floats to the top of the pot. After a couple of hours, dip a ladle deep into the pot so you can taste the actual broth and not the fat floating on top. Add a little salt to the ladle and taste the broth. If it's pleasingly chicken-flavored, the broth is done. If not, allow the birds to cook another half hour or so.

STRAIN THE BROTH   Remove the chicken and strain the broth several times through a chinois or other fine strainer. Cool the broth in the refrigerator. Once cooled, the fat will float to the top; remove about 90 percent of this fat. (A little fat is good for flavor.) Use the broth within a few days or freeze it.

2 whole chickens, 3 to 4 pounds each, giblets removed, rinsed inside and out, breasts removed and saved for another dish

1 carrot, cut into 6 to 8 pieces

1 celery stalk, cut into 6 to 8 pieces

1 small onion, peeled and quartered

3 to 4 fresh thyme sprigs

Kosher salt

CHICKEN REDUCTION MAKES ABOUT 1 QUART

Essentially a brown chicken stock reduced until full bodied and intensely flavorful, this reduction adds body as well as deep flavor to sauces and braises. Freeze it in varying amounts so you can easily pull out just the amount called for in a recipe. In recipes that call for this reduction, you can substitute a good-quality purchased product, such as the Glace de Poulet Gold made by More Than Gourmet. (Dilute it with water until a little thicker than chicken stock before using it.) The final flavor of the dish will be a little different with this product (not bad, just different), but you will get the important textural benefit from it.

6 pounds uncooked chicken bones, some meat still on is fine

3 tablespoons extra virgin olive oil

1 medium onion, coarsely chopped

1 garlic clove, coarsely chopped

1 carrot, coarsely chopped

2 celery stalks, coarsely chopped

4 whole canned tomatoes (about 4 ounces), coarsely chopped

4 fresh rosemary sprigs, bruised with the dull side of a chef's knife

2 cups dry white wine

ROAST THE BONES   Heat the oven to 425°F. Rinse the chicken bones and pat them dry. Spread them out in a single layer with a little room between the bones on one large or two smaller sheet pans. Roast until they are golden brown, about 1 hour, flipping and turning the bones every 15 minutes or so.

MAKE THE STOCK   In a large stockpot, heat the olive oil over medium heat. Add the onion, garlic, carrot, and celery and cook, stirring occasionally, until the vegetables are well browned, about 20 minutes. Add the tomatoes, rosemary, wine, and bones to the stockpot. Add enough water to cover everything by about 2 inches (6 to 8 quarts). Cook over medium heat (you want a gentle simmer, not a boil) until the stock has a full flavor, about 1½ hours.

Remove the chicken bones and strain the broth several times through a chinois or other fine strainer. If you want to use the reduction right away, spoon off any visible fat floating on top of the stock.

Otherwise, chill the stock until the fat solidifies on top and then scrape off and discard most of it.

REDUCE THE STOCK   Pour the defatted stock into a saucepan and bring to a boil over high heat, then reduce the heat slightly so the stock is not boiling so furiously. As the stock reduces, it will glaze the sides of the saucepan; use a spoon or ladle to pour some of the stock over the sides to deglaze the pan. (This will further increase the intensity of the flavor.) Continue simmering until the stock has darkened and reduced to about 1 quart, 45 minutes to an hour. Use right away, refrigerate for up to 3 days, or freeze.

LOBSTER BROTH MAKES ABOUT 7 CUPS

This flavorful shellfish and tomato broth can be used in most seafood recipes where chicken broth is called for. It's especially delicious in the lobster recipes in this book, particularly Lobster Risotto (page 117). Gather cooked lobster shells as you use whole lobster, freeze the shells, and then make this stock when you have a pound of them. (Your fishmonger may also have spent lobster shells that he's willing to part with.)

1 tablespoon extra virgin olive oil

1 onion, sliced

Pinch of crushed red pepper flakes

One 14.5-ounce can tomatoes, drained, seeded, and chopped (about 1½ cups)

1 pound lobster shells (from about 2 cooked lobsters), coarsely chopped

2 cups dry white wine

About 12 basil leaves, coarsely chopped

In a large soup pot, heat the olive oil over medium heat. Add the onion and cook, stirring occasionally, until soft, about 12 minutes. Add the red pepper flakes, tomatoes, and lobster shells. Increase the heat to medium-high and cook, stirring occasionally for another few minutes. Add the wine, bring it to a boil, and let it cook until reduced by about half. Add 2 quarts of water to the pot, bring it to a boil, reduce to a simmer, and cook for 40 minutes, until reduced by half. Add the basil and cook for another minute before straining the broth through a mesh strainer. Use the broth immediately, refrigerate it for up to 3 days, or freeze it. Season it with salt and pepper as you use it.

SOURCES

Nowadays, finding a source for a specialty product is just a mouse click away. Below are some of my favorite sources for good-quality Italian and hard-to-find ingredients.

A. G. FERRARI (www.agferrari.com; 877/878–2783) carries all kinds of Italian ingredients, including specialty pastas and a wide selection of truffle products.

BUON ITALIA, which has a retail outlet in Chelsea Market in New York City, carries many fine Italian products, including my favorite all-purpose brand of vinegar, Trucioleto, and burrata cheese. Visit them at www.buonitalia.com or call 212/633–9090.

CHEF'S WAREHOUSE, www.chefswarehouse.com, is a great resource for all kinds of ingredients such as high-quality dried pasta, fresh white truffles, and Italian cheeses, but many items come in bulk sizes only.

FORMAGGIO KITCHEN, which has retail stores in Boston and Cambridge, Massachusetts, sells artisanal Italian cheeses as well as high-quality anchovies, capers, polenta, pasta, fregola, and preserves. Visit them online at www.formaggiokitchen.com or call 888/212–3224.

MORE THAN GOURMET makes all kinds of reduced sauces, including the Glace de Poulet Gold that I recommend in place of my own chicken reduction. The sauces are available at some gourmet groceries and through the company's Web site: www.morethan gourmet.com.

MURRAY'S CHEESE, based in Manhattan on Bleecker Street with an outpost in Grand Central Market, is my favorite source for cheese. For mail order, call 888/692–4339 or visit www.murrays cheese.com.

SALUMERIA BIELLESE (212/736–7376), in New York City, has outstanding cured meats.

URBANI TRUFFLES is a great source for truffles and truffle products as well as high-quality wild mushrooms (www.urbani.com; 800/281–2330).

INDEX

Puree
about pureeing, 10
asparagus, seared bass with asparagus
potato cakes and, **136**, 137–139
basil, orecchiette with green beans,
potatoes, and, 104
pea, springtime soft-shell crab with, **152**,
153–154
spinach, shirred eggs in, 62
sunchoke and caramelized shallot, mixed
seafood stufato with, 29–30
zucchini, 132; crispy skate with pan-
roasted potatoes, caper salmoriglio,
and, 131–133

Q

Quail, 157
grilled, with shallots, grapes, walnuts, and
creamy polenta, 172–173

R

Rabbit, 157
braised, with herbed spaetzle, caramelized
parsnips, and mint, 174–176
Radicchio
breaded veal chops and, with prosciutto-
balsamic sauce, 194–195
smoked ham, roasted radicchio, and
cheese panini, **72–73**, 74
Ragu
duck, pappardelle with black olives and,
87–88
sausage and polenta, 181
Raisin and pine nut *mostarda*, La Tur with,
234
Ramps
herbed goat cheese and ramp salad,
41
Raviolini, ricotta, 92–93
with anchovy butter and zucchini, 91
Raw shellfish with cucumber and tomato
salad, 36

Red pepper, 6
chile oil, 27; oysters with blood orange,
smoked sea salt, and, 26
Red snapper
moist-roasted whole red snapper with
tomatoes, basil, and oregano,
148–149, **150–151**
roasted, with summer squash and cipollini
agrodolce (substitute), 141–142
Reduction, chicken, 242–243
Red wine sauce, venison with seared bacon
and shallot dumplings and, 203–205
Rib eye of beef with kale and bluefoot
mushrooms, **184**, 185–186
Ribs
braised spareribs with Tyrolean potatoes
and artichokes, 182–183
short ribs and fregola with corn and
butternut squash, 187–188
Ricotta
with lemon and poppy seed marmalade,
235
raviolini, 92–93; with anchovy butter and
zucchini, 91
Ricotta salata, marinated cucumber salad
with, 48
Riesling, chilled pea soup with crab,
tarragon, and, 57
Risotto, 107–120
basic recipe, 107
chicken liver and spinach, 119–120
fava bean, with morels, pecorino, and
balsamic vinegar, 113–114
lobster, 117–118
rock shrimp, with spring vegetables and
crispy shallots, 115–116
sweet potato, braised oxtail and, 108–112,
110–111
Robiola cheese, roasted baby beet salad with
Banyuls vinaigrette and, **44**, 45
Rocher (crispy chocolate bites), 217
Rock shrimp risotto with spring vegetables
and crispy shallots, 115–116
Root vegetables. *See also specific types*
roasted, 163; boneless roast chicken with,
162

Rosemary
chickpea soup with sausage, cabbage,
and, 58–59
cranberry bean soup with pancetta and,
56
herb- and garlic-infused tomatoes, 21
light and crispy fritto misto with fried
lemons and herbs, **22**, 23–24
rosemary-scented olives, 16
whole roast chicken *in potacchio*, 161
Rutabaga
roasted root vegetables, 163; boneless
roast chicken with, 162

S

Saffron gelato, 219
Salad(s), 40–48
about, 39
artichoke "panzanella," lemon and garlic
sardines with, 37
Campari citrus salad with orange custard
"French toast," 224–225
crab, chilled, with ginger and chives, 65
crispy sweetbreads salad, 70–71
cucumber and tomato, raw shellfish
with, 36
grilled eggplant, marinated tomato, and
arugula, 42–43
grilled salmon, corn, and avocado, 66
herbed goat cheese and ramp salad, 41
marinated cucumber salad with ricotta
salata, 48
mixed greens with marinated cherry
tomatoes and shallots, 40
preserved tuna and potato, 68
roasted baby beet salad with Robiola
cheese and Banyuls vinaigrette,
44, 45
sliced artichoke salad, 46, **47**
tomato and arugula, 200; grilled
butterflied leg of lamb with, 199
Salmon
grilled salmon, corn, and avocado salad,
66

Turbot with caramelized endive, lentils, and
    salsa verde, 143–144, **145**
Turnips
    roasted root vegetables, 163; boneless
        roast chicken with, 162
    slow-roasted salmon with trumpet
        mushrooms and, 140
Tyrolean potatoes and artichokes, 183
    braised spareribs with, 182–183

V

Vanilla gelato, 219
Veal
    breaded veal chops and radicchio with
        prosciutto-balsamic sauce, 194–195
Vegetables
    about blanching, 9–10, 11
    roasted root vegetables, 163; boneless
        roast chicken with, 162
    sautéed summer vegetables, 191; beef
        tenderloin with pearl onion agrodolce
        and, 189–190
    spring, rock shrimp risotto with crispy
        shallots and, 115–116

Venison with red wine sauce, with seared
    bacon and shallot dumplings, 203–205
Vinaigrette
    Banyuls, roasted baby beet salad with
        Robiola cheese and, **44**, 45
    gazpacho, spicy grilled shrimp with, 28

W

Walnuts
    grilled quail with shallots, grapes, creamy
        polenta, and, 172–173
    walnut-currant bread, 238–239
Winter squash
    fregola with corn and butternut squash,
        188
    short ribs and, 187–188
    penne with roasted pumpkin, escarole,
        and mushrooms, 81
    squash and fruit panzanella, 165–166;
        rustic braised chicken with, 164–165
    sweet and spicy roasted butternut squash,
        180; spice-coated pork loin with
        butternut squash and wilted arugula,
        178–179

whole roast chicken with pumpkin,
    mushrooms, and ginger, 160

Z

Zabaglione, thyme, puff pastry apricot
    "tatin" with, 214–216, **215**
Zucchini
    fritto misto, light and crispy, with fried
        lemons and herbs, **22**, 23–24
    puree, 132; crispy skate with pan-roasted
        potatoes, caper salmoriglio, and,
        131–133
    ricotta raviolini with anchovy butter and,
        91–93
    roasted orata with summer squash and
        cipollini agrodolce, 141–142
    sautéed summer vegetables, 191; beef
        tenderloin with pearl onion agrodolce
        and, 189–190
    smoky beef and potato stew with
        cauliflower, spinach, fontina cheese,
        and, 192–193

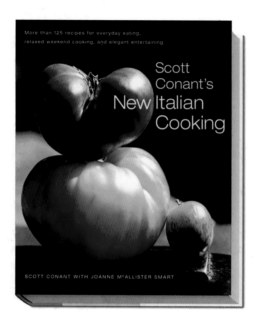